MICKEY ROGERS
JOANNE TAYLORE-KNOWLES
STEVE TAYLORE-KNOWLES

SPEAK YOUR MIND

STUDENT'S BOOK
+ access to Student's App and Digital Workbook

1A

macmillan education

SCOPE & SEQUENCE

	Outcomes	Vocabulary	Grammar	Speaking
Unit 1 Who Are You? pp. 7–15	• Describe who you are and what you like in an online profile • Greet and introduce people in various settings • Complete registration information with numbers	• Forms • Greetings, introductions, and goodbyes • Ordinal numbers	• *Be* statements and *yes/no* questions • Information questions with *be* Grammar Reference pp. 142–143	• Describe people • Make introductions • Give personal information
	Language and Life—Communication: Make an Interesting Online Profile			
Unit 2 Work/Life Balance pp. 17–25	• Talk about various jobs • Talk about members of your family • Discuss your family members and their jobs	• Work life • Family • Jobs	• Articles *a*, *an*, and no article • Possessive adjectives and *'s/s'* Grammar Reference pp. 143–144	• Talk about a famous person • Talk about family • Describe a picture
	Language and Life—Self-awareness: Find the Right Job for Your Interests and Abilities			
Unit 3 Fun and Games pp. 27–35	• Express likes and dislikes • Talk about and recommend free-time activities • Plan and talk about an event	• Likes and dislikes • Free-time activities • Special events	• Simple present statements and *yes/no* questions • The imperative Grammar Reference pp. 145–146	• Talk about things you like to do • Recommend free-time activities • Describe an event
	Language and Life—Creativity: Create an Interest Group for a Website			
Unit 4 That's Life! pp. 37–45	• Talk about daily activities • Talk about how often you do activities • Describe your day off	• Daily activities • Frequency and time expressions • Routine activities	• Simple present information questions • Frequency adverbs Grammar Reference pp. 146–147	• Interview a partner about daily activities • Talk about routine activities • Discuss the perfect day off
	Language and Life—Adaptability: Give Advice about Keeping Life Interesting			
Unit 5 Finding Your Way pp. 47–55	• Talk about places to live • Describe your neighborhood • Give directions	• Where you live • Places in a neighborhood • Directions	• Adjectives • *There is / There are* Grammar Reference pp. 148–149	• Talk about where you live • Discuss a neighborhood • Give directions
	Language and Life—Problem-solving: Create a Guide to Your Neighborhood			
Unit 6 Going Viral pp. 57–65	• Talk about social media use • Talk about computer equipment and vlogging • Talk about buying and selling online	• Emotions • Technology equipment • Technology phrases	• Present progressive • Present progressive vs. simple present Grammar Reference pp. 149–150	• Talk about routines and feelings • Discuss vlogs • Discuss online activity
	Language and Life—Critical Thinking: Analyze the Pros and Cons of A Digital Detox			

Confident Communicator	Pronunciation	Listening/Reading	Thinking Skills	Writing
Repair It • Ask for repetition *Start Talking* • Add details *Start Talking* • Useful phrases	• Intonation in *yes/no* and information questions	Read a social media profile • Skill—Infer information Listen to short conversations of greetings • Skill—Listen for details Listen for personal details • Skill—Listen for numerical information	• Evaluate • Deduce	Write about a school calendar
Unit Review p. 16 **Study Skills** p. 127—Memory Strategies				
Keep Talking • Useful phrases *Repair It* • Check for understanding *Keep Talking* • Use notes	• *An* + vowel	Read an online article about a business owner • Skill—Scan Listen to a conversation about a family picture • Skill—Use visual clues Listen to a description of a family vacation picture • Skill—Predict	• Question • Analyze • Categorize	Write an online family profile
Unit Review p. 26 **Follow A Pro** p. 128—An IT Consultant ▶ An IT Professional				
Keep Talking • Emphasize preference *Keep Talking* • Give reasons *Keep Talking* • Express rules	• Third person –s	Read a magazine interview • Skill—Infer Listen to a phone conversation about an event • Skill—Take notes Listen to a recorded advertisement • Skill—Listen for gist	• Categorize • Understand • Recall	Create a poster to advertise a special event
Unit Review p. 36 **Study Skills** p. 129—Oral Presentations				
Start Talking • Give examples *Keep Talking* • Useful phrases *Keep Talking* • Express frequency	• Word stress in information questions	Read a blog post about a reporter's day • Skill—Scan Listen to an interview with an actress • Skill—Listen for specific information Listen to a radio show about daily routines • Skill—Listen for gist	• Analyze • Summarize • Recall	Write about the perfect day off
Unit Review p. 46 **Follow A Pro** p. 130—A Firefighter ▶ A Paramedic				
Keep Talking • Make guesses *Keep Talking* • Useful phrases *Start Talking* • Useful phrases	• Syllable stress in multi-syllable adjectives	Read an article about unusual places to live • Skill—Scan for specific information Listen to a radio show about neighborhoods • Skill—Listen for specific information Listen to conversations asking for directions • Skill—Listen for key words	• Apply • Evaluate • Analyze	Write an instant message
Unit Review p. 56 **Study Skills** p. 131—Research Skills				
Start Talking • Useful phrases *Keep Talking* • Show interest *Keep Talking* • Ask follow-up questions	• /ŋ/	Read an article about social media use and employment • Skill—Predict information Listen to vloggers describe their videos • Skill—Listen for fact and opinion Listen to an internet business owner • Skill—Listen for the main idea	• Analyze • Evaluate	Write a social media ad
Unit Review p. 66 **Follow A Pro** p. 132—A Chief Listening Officer ▶ A Social Media Manager				

Grammar Quiz: What Do You Already Know?

A Choose the correct option.

1 I'm am not / I'm not / I isn't Brazilian.
2 Am / Is / Are your teacher from Peru?
3 It's / It / It not nice to meet you.
4 Where be / is / are they from?
5 What is / are / does your last name?
6 We am / is / are not Spanish students.

B Complete the paragraph with the simple present form of the verbs in parentheses.

Many students **1** ____________ (not know) what they want to do after they finish college. But I do. I **2** ____________ (want) to be a flight attendant. Flight attendants **3** ____________ (travel) the world, and I **4** ____________ (love) to travel! My friend Beth **5** ____________ (work) as a flight attendant now. She **6** ____________ (not make) a lot of money, but she's happy.

C Complete the sentences with the present progressive form of the verbs in the box.

cook not do not listen rain wear work

1 It ____________ outside. Don't forget to take your umbrella.
2 The teacher is angry because the students ____________.
3 Harry has a great job. He ____________ at the office in Spain right now.
4 Sorry, I can't talk right now. I ____________ dinner.
5 Calvin ____________ the laundry now because he doesn't have any soap.
6 Dan ____________ shorts and a T-shirt because it's very hot today.

D Unscramble and write sentences.

1 listen / we / to / sometimes / music / .
____
2 I / where / vegetables / buy / can / ?
____
3 never / is / our / teacher / late / .
____
4 hair / long / Sally / has / brown / .
____
5 there / many / eggs / how / are / ?
____
6 cook / does / Adam / how / often / ?
____

E Find one error in each sentence. Write the correct sentence.

1 My fathers' name is Antonio.
____
2 Please take a umbrella with you.
____
3 Why do you have three cell phone?
____
4 Don't to forget to come to my party.
____
5 Jeff take the train to work.
____
6 We have any tomatoes.
____

Go to the Grammar Review on pages 140–141.

UNIT 1

Who Are You?

WHAT DO YOU ALREADY KNOW?

1 Think of words you know that describe you. Write the words.

2 IN PAIRS Share and compare your words. If possible, add more words to the box.

I am ...

VIDEO

DISCUSS & SHARE

3 IN GROUPS Watch the video and answer the question.

SYM Are you typical or different?

In this unit, you will ...

- describe yourself, introduce yourself and others, and give personal details about yourself.
- use thinking skills: evaluate and draw conclusions.
- read about a social media profile.
- use strategies to start talking and keep talking by asking for repetition or asking for details.
- use communication skills to create an interesting social media profile.
- learn strategies for memorization.

LESSON 1 About You

READING

A Are you on any social media sites? Which ones? Discuss.

B **1.01 READING SKILL—Infer information** Read the form. Then choose the correct answer.

International English Teachers

Your Profile

ABOUT YOU

I'm an English teacher in Germany. I'm from Berlin. I speak German, English, and Spanish. My hobbies are swimming, dancing, and yoga. My favorite music is rock and my favorite food is tacos (♥ Mexican food). My boyfriend is Juan. He isn't an English teacher. He's a yoga teacher.

Username:	Berliner100	Last name:	Steiner
Password:	DerSeestern!	Nickname:	Angie
Re-enter password:	DerSeestern!	Date of birth:	04/15/97
First name:	Angela	Country:	Germany

Edit Profile

1 Is this an English-language website? Yes, it is. / No, it isn't.
2 Is Angie Steiner the name on her passport? Yes, it is. / No, it isn't.
3 Is the number 04 a month? Yes, it is. / No, it isn't.
4 Is she from Europe? Yes, she is. / No, she isn't.
5 Is she a yoga teacher? Yes, she is. / No, she isn't.
6 Is she married? Yes, she is. / No, she isn't.

C **THINKING SKILL—Evaluate** Consider why some passwords are secure and others are not secure.

VOCABULARY

A Match the personal information (1–6) to a category (a–f). Write the letter.

1 11/18/90 ____	**a** last name
2 Robert ____	**b** nickname
3 US ____	**c** hobby
4 Garcia ____	**d** date of birth
5 playing video games ____	**e** first name
6 Robbie ____	**f** country

B Complete the profile for you. Then share with a partner.

First name ____________	Date of birth ____________
Last name ____________	Country ____________
Nickname ____________	Hobbies ____________

A: My first name is Amanda. And you?

B: My first name is Olivia. My last name is …

GRAMMAR *be statements and yes/no questions*

A IN PAIRS **Complete the examples.**

Affirmative	Negative
1 I ______ / I'm an English teacher. **2** We are / We'______ English students. **3** He ______ / He's a yoga teacher.	**4** I am not / I'm ______ from Mexico. **5** They are not / They're not / They ______ German teachers. **6** He is not / He's not / He ______ an English teacher.

Questions and Short Answers

7 Are you late? Yes, I am. / No, I'm ______.
8 Is she married? Yes, she ______. / No, she's not. / No, she isn't.
9 Are they from Berlin? Yes, they are. / No, ______ not. / No, they aren't.

For more practice, go to page 142.

B **Complete with the correct forms of *be*.**

1. ______ you a student? No, I ______. I ______ a teacher.
2. ______ your parents from Mexico? No, they ______. They ______ from Brazil.
3. ______ your English teacher American? Yes, he ______.
4. ______ I in the correct classroom? No, you ______. This ______ English 5.

C **Complete the answers for you.**

1. Are you on social media?
   Yes, I'm on two social media sites.
2. Is your favorite hobby playing video games?
   ______
3. Is your favorite food from your country?
   ______
4. Are your parents from this city?
   ______

MAKE IT REAL

Informal ways to say *Yes: Yeah, Uh-huh, Yep*
Informal ways to say *No: Uh-uh, Nope, No way*

D IN PAIRS **Ask and answer the questions in C.**

SPEAKING

A **Complete the survey for you.**

About me ...

From	Nickname	Favorite food
Hobbies	Birth month	Favorite music

B IN GROUPS **Ask questions and try to guess your partner's answers. Use the Confident Communicator box to help you.**

A: Are you from Brazil? *B: No, I'm not.*
C: Are you from Mexico? *B: Yes, I am.*

CONFIDENT COMMUNICATOR
REPAIR IT

When you don't understand or don't hear something, ask for repetition.
Excuse me?
Sorry, can you repeat that, please?

Hello and Goodbye

LISTENING

A **Look at the pictures (a–c). Match the pictures to the questions (1–4).**

a

b

c

1 How do you greet a good friend or a family member? ______
2 How do you greet a new classmate? ______
3 How do you greet an important person for the first time? ______
4 How do you greet someone you don't know well? ______

B 1.02 THINKING SKILL—Deduce **Listen. Check (✓) if the people know each other.**

1 ☐ Sandy and Jake
2 ☐ Janice Walters and Lynn Jefferson
3 ☐ Mr. Wilson and Sarah
4 ☐ Christine, Mark, and Jean Luc

C 1.02 LISTENING SKILL—Listen for details **Listen again and choose the correct answer.**

1 Where is Michelle?
a at work
b at home
c with Jake

2 Who is the office manager?
a Lynn
b Ms. Jefferson
c Janice

3 Why is Mr. Wilson at DT Bank?
a to work
b to talk about his account
c to get money

4 What country is Jean Luc from?
a France
b the US
c Canada

VOCABULARY greetings, introductions, and goodbyes

A **Complete the table with phrases from the box.**

Bye.	Good morning.	Hey!
~~Hi.~~	How's it going?	~~I'm John Smith.~~
Nice to meet you.	See you later.	How are you?
~~Take care.~~	This is Nicolle Martin.	It's nice to meet you.

MAKE IT YOURS

Can you think of situations when you have to introduce someone in English?

Greetings	Introductions	Goodbyes
Hi.	*I'm John Smith.*	*Take care.*

B **Complete the conversation with words and phrases from A.**

Kara: **1** ____________, Josie. How's **2** ____________?

Josie: **3** ____________, Kara. I'm good. **4** ____________?

Kara: Fine, thanks. Josie, **5** ____________ my friend Michelle Kim.

Josie: Hi, Michelle. I'm Josie Grayson. It's **6** ____________.

Michelle: **7** ____________, too, Josie.

Kara: Well, it's good to see you, Josie. **8** ____________.

Josie: Nice to see you, too. **9** ____________.

MAKE IT REAL

In informal situations, people use very short and informal forms of greetings and goodbyes.

Greetings:	Goodbyes:
What's up?	*Later!*
How you doing?	*Catch you later.*
What's new?	*See ya!*

C **IN GROUPS** **Practice the conversation in B using your own names.**

GRAMMAR information questions with *be*

A **Complete the table with *what, where, when,* or *how*.**

Question Word + *be* + Word or Phrase	Answer
Who is your teacher?	Mr. Oliver is my teacher.
1 ________ is your name?	My name is Lisette.
2 ________ is Mandy?	She's at the office in Chicago.
3 ________ is your birthday?	It's in May.
4 ________ are you?	I'm fine, thanks.

For more practice, go to page 142.

B **Complete the questions and answers for you.**

1 ____________'s your name? It's ________________________.
2 ____________ old are you? I'm ________________________.
3 ____________ are you from? I'm from ________________________.
4 ____________ is your birthday? It's in ________________________. (month)
5 ____________ is your favorite singer? My favorite singer is ________________________.

C **IN PAIRS** **Ask and answer the questions in B.**

SPEAKING

A **IN GROUPS** **Greet classmates you know. Introduce yourself to classmates you do not know. Ask questions to find out more information about each person.**

A: Hi. I'm Sal. How's it going?
B: Great. I'm Leslie. How are you, Sal?
A: Fine, thanks. Where are you from?
B: I'm from Port-au-Prince, Haiti. Where are you from?

B **Introduce someone to your class. The person you introduce then introduces someone else. Use the Confident Communicator box to help you.**

CONFIDENT COMMUNICATOR
START TALKING

When we introduce someone, it is common to give a little more information about the person.
This is Robert. He's my neighbor. He's from Chicago.

LESSON 3 Numbers

VOCABULARY ordinal numbers

A 1.03 Write the ordinal numbers for the days of the month.

APRIL						
SUNDAY	MONDAY	TUESDAY	WEDNESDAY	THURSDAY	FRIDAY	SATURDAY
	1 first	2 second	3 third	4 fourth	5 fifth	6 sixth
7 seventh	8 eighth	9 ninth	10 tenth	11 eleventh	12 twelfth	13 thirteenth
14 fourteenth	15 fifteenth	16 1 ________	17 seventeenth	18 eighteenth	19 nineteenth	20 twentieth
21 2 ________	22 3 ________	23 twenty-third	24 twenty-fourth	25 twenty-fifth	26 twenty-sixth	27 4 ________
28 5 ________	29 twenty-ninth	30 thirtieth				

B IN PAIRS Complete the sentences for you. Then discuss.

1 My birthday is ____________.

2 Today is ____________.

3 New Year's Day is ____________.

4 My favorite holiday is ____________, on ____________.

5 In my family, I am the ____________ child.

LISTENING

A IN PAIRS THINKING SKILL—Evaluate Make a list of dates that are important to you. Ask your partner why his/her dates are important.

A: Why is August 2 important to you? Is it your birthday? *B: Yes, it is.*

B 1.04 LISTENING SKILL—Listen for numerical information Listen to the conversation and answer the questions.

MAKE IT REAL

Write dates with cardinal numbers: April 4.
Say dates with ordinal numbers: April fourth (4th).
US: write dates as month, day, year: 10/22/2019.
UK: write dates as day, month, year: 22/10/19.

1 What is Olivia's date of birth? ____________

2 What is her address? ____________

3 Is her phone number 555-376-5832? ____________

4 How much money is the registration? ____________

5 When does Olivia's group start? ____________

6 Is this her first marathon? ____________

PRONUNCIATION intonation in *yes/no* and information questions

A 1.04 Listen again. Draw an arrow pointing up if the speaker's voice goes up at the end of the question. Draw an arrow pointing down if the speaker's voice goes down at the end of the question.

What is your first name? ↘ *Is registration open?* ↗

1 What's your last name?
2 And your phone number?
3 What is your date of birth?
4 Is this your first marathon?

B IN PAIRS Ask and answer the questions from A. Use correct intonation for *yes/no* and information questions.

WRITING

A Read the rules for capital letters. Then correct the capitalization mistakes in the text.

Capitalize:
- names of people, pets, places: Daniel, San Francisco, my cat Coco
- countries, nationalities, languages: Ecuador, British, Chinese
- months, days, holidays: January, Monday, Independence Day
- the pronoun *I*
- the first letter of the first word in a sentence

Adams English Academy Academic Calendar

August 21–September 2	registration opens
September 2	fall semester begins
December 10	fall semester ends
December 15–January 5	school closed
January 6–10	registration opens
January 11	spring semester begins

i am a student at Adams english Academy. Registration is from August 21st to September 2nd. The first day of class is on September 2nd. The first semester is from September 2nd to December 10th. The school is closed from December 15th to January 5th for the new Year holiday. the next semester is from january 11th to May 3rd. I'm in the first level, and my teacher is Robert green. His nickname is rob.

B Write about your English class or school. Use the paragraph in A as a model. Remember to use capital letters.

SPEAKING

A IN PAIRS Read the questions out loud and answer them as quickly as you can. Use the Confident Communicator box to help you.

1 What is the eighth month of the year? ____________
2 What is the fourteenth letter of the English alphabet? ____________
3 What is the day after the last day of the year? ____________
4 What is two days after the second day of the weekend? ____________
5 What is the extra day in February? ____________
6 What is the 365th day of the year? ____________
7 Write your own: ____________

B IN GROUPS Check your answers. How many pairs got 100% correct?

CONFIDENT COMMUNICATOR
START TALKING

To talk about numbers in math, say:
+ plus – minus × times ÷ divided by = equals
Five plus two equals seven, and five minus three equals two.

Language and Life

Communication – Online Profiles

A **1.05 Read the online article. Choose *True* or *False*.**

SOCIAL MEDIA PROFILE TIPS

Many social media websites have different parts in the personal profile section.

One part is often about specific preferences—movies, books, TV shows, and sports. Another part is for biographical information. When you create a social media profile, here are some things to consider:

- Are your preferences interesting?
- Is your personal information interesting? Write one or two interesting things about yourself!
- Is your information safe? Don't write your home address, phone number, or vacation dates.
- Are your grammar and spelling correct? Your language is part of your reputation!
- Finally, is your picture good? Use a clear picture of yourself.

1	This is a social media website.	True / False
2	Many social media profiles have different sections.	True / False
3	Your entertainment preferences are a part of your personality.	True / False
4	It's a good idea to include your phone number and address in your profile.	True / False
5	Grammar and spelling are not important in a social media profile.	True / False

B **IN PAIRS Help Amanda improve her profile. Circle and correct five capitalization errors and one grammar error.**

SYM INSTITUTE

HOME | CALENDAR | FACULTY | STAFF | ORGANIZATION | STUDENT PROFILES

Basics

Name: Amanda herrero
Age: 20
Hometown: Recife
English level or class: 1B (Beginner)

Interests/Favorites

Music/Musicians: pop—Ed Sheeran, Camila Cabello; reggaeton
Games: *League of Legends*
People I like: Beyoncé, Bill and Melinda Gates, Neymar
Hobbies: dancing, going out to eat, beach parties
Other: my cats, my boyfriend julio

More About Me

I'm a student in communications at the Federal university of Pernambuco, in recife. My favorite Things is my pets and my car (an old Volkswagen Beetle!).

C **Circle two things for Amanda to add to the Basics section and three things for her to add to the Interests/Favorites section.**

Basics	
Address	Email address
Birthday	Hair and eye color
Brothers and sisters	Phone number
Country	Social media sites

Interests/Favorites	
Actors	Movies
Animals	Places
Apps	Sports
Clothes	TV shows
Food/restaurants	

D **Write questions Amanda can use as ideas for the More About Me section.**

Who's your favorite person in the world?
What is your favorite animal?

1 ______________________________
2 ______________________________
3 ______________________________
4 ______________________________
5 ______________________________

E **Complete a profile for you.**

HOME | CALENDAR | FACULTY | STAFF | ORGANIZATION | STUDENT PROFILES

Upload Photo

Basics
Name: ______________________________
Age: ______________________________
Hometown: ______________________________
English level or class: ______________________________

Interests/Favorites
Music/Musicians: ______________________________
Games: ______________________________
People: ______________________________
Social activities: ______________________________
Other: ______________________________

More About Me
____
____
____
____
____

F **IN PAIRS** **Read your partner's profile. Make suggestions to improve the profile. Does your partner …**

capitalize words correctly?	Yes / No
use *be* correctly?	Yes / No
describe herself/himself?	Yes / No

MAKE IT DIGITAL

Join an English-language social media site. Use some of the ideas in this lesson to create your profile.

VOCABULARY review

SCORE: / 10

A Complete the paragraph with words from the box.

favorite first food hello hobbies hometown meet nice nickname up

1 ____________! What's **2** ____________? My name is Manuel. My **3** ____________ is Manny. I'm from El Salvador. My **4** ____________ is Santa Ana. I'm 16 and a student. My **5** ____________ are swimming and playing soccer. My **6** ____________ music is pop and my favorite **7** ____________ is pizza. My birthday is August **8** ____________. It's **9** ____________ to **10** ____________ you!

GRAMMAR review

SCORE: / 10

A Unscramble the sentences. Use the correct form of *be*.

1 from Brazil / my parents / be / . ____________

2 I / on social media / not / be / . ____________

3 teachers / they / be / ? ____________

4 last name / your / Stevens / be / ? ____________

5 I / your English class / in / be / ? ____________

B Complete the questions.

1	____________ your name?	My name's Celia.
2	____________ it going?	Great, thanks.
3	____________ you from?	I'm from Medellin, Colombia.
4	____________ your birthday?	It's July 3.
5	____________ your favorite singer?	Ariana Grande.

16–20 correct: You can talk about greetings and ordinal numbers. You can use *be* statements and information questions.
0–15 correct: Look again at the Vocabulary and Grammar sections in the unit.

TOTAL SCORE: / 20

WHAT DO YOU KNOW NOW? Look back at page 7 and add the words you know now to the box.

STUDY SKILLS MEMORY STRATEGIES

Take the quiz about memory strategies. Go to **Study Skills** on page 127 to find the answers. Then learn more about memory strategies.

1 Left-handed people have better memories.
a true **b** false

2 Which foods help your memory?
a chicken and potatoes **b** vegetables, fruit, and nuts **c** cheese and chocolate

3 What is a good way to help you remember things?
a Sleep after studying. **b** Exercise before studying. **c** Drink coffee when you study.

4 It is possible for students to learn … new words per hour of study.
a 1–5 **b** 5–10 **c** 10–20

UNIT 2 Work/Life Balance

WHAT DO YOU ALREADY KNOW?

1 Think about your day and the things you do at school or work, with family, and with friends. Write the activities and the percentage of time you do the activities each week.

2 **IN PAIRS** Share and compare your activities. Think of more words to add to each category.

School or work __%

Family __%

Friends __%

DISCUSS & SHARE

VIDEO

3 **IN GROUPS** Watch the video and answer the question.

SYM Is it possible to have a good work and life balance?

In this unit, you will ...

- talk about jobs, members of your family, and what jobs they do.
- use thinking skills: hypothesize, infer, and categorize.
- read about a young woman entrepreneur.
- use strategies to repair talking by checking for understanding.
- use notes when you speak in front of the class.
- use self-awareness skills to evaluate your interests and abilities for a job.
- follow an IT professional to learn about this job and the skills needed for this industry.

In Business

READING

A Are you (or a member of your family) a business owner? What business is it? Discuss.

B 2.01 Read the article. Then discuss the questions.

A Woman at Work Zinah Saleh, Iraq

Zinah Saleh is a **business owner** with a **successful** business. She is the owner of her **company**, Ishtar Handmade Soap. Her company makes eco-friendly soap and shampoo. The all-natural soap **products** are very popular. All of the products use olive oil from Iraq. They also use fruit from trees in Africa.

Female business owners are unusual in Iraq. Zinah has a degree in business administration, and she wants to help women find jobs. Zinah's **employees** are all women. There are female soap makers, **administrators**, and **marketers**. Zinah's parents are happy for her. Her father is an engineer and her mother is a homemaker. Zinah thinks working women are important for her country's economy.

Read more

1 Where is Zinah Saleh from?
2 What is her job?
3 What is Zinah's business?
4 What is in the Ishtar products?
5 What is unusual about Zinah's company?

C READING SKILL—Scan **Read the article quickly and underline the jobs.**

D THINKING SKILL—Question **Why do you think eco-friendly products are popular? Are eco-friendly products important to you? Discuss.**

VOCABULARY

A Find words from the article that match the definitions. Write the word.

1 another word for business ______
2 people who advertise products ______
3 people who work for a business owner ______
4 people who manage the paperwork of a business ______
5 a person who has a business ______
6 things that a business sells ______

B List eight adjectives from the article.

______ ______ ______ ______
______ ______ ______ ______

GRAMMAR articles a, an, and no article

A Choose the correct option to complete the rules.

1 The words *a* and *an* come before singular / plural nouns.
2 *A* comes before a noun that starts with a vowel / consonant.
3 *An* comes before a noun that starts with a vowel / consonant.
4 In adjective + noun phrases, *a/an* comes before the adjective / noun.
5 If a noun is plural, use *a* / *an* / no article.

For more practice, go to page 143.

B Complete with *a*, *an*, or *X* (no article).

1 _____ homemaker is an important job.
2 There are _____ social media marketers at online companies.
3 I think business owners have _____ exciting jobs.
4 A lot of women in my country are _____ business owners.
5 I prefer _____ creative job, like _____ art teacher or _____ music teacher.
6 Math is important to be _____ engineer or _____ architect.

MAKE IT YOURS

Make a list of local businesses in your area. What products or services do the businesses sell?

C IN PAIRS Read the sentences in B. Are they true, in your opinion?

PRONUNCIATION *an* + vowel

A 2.02 Listen and notice how phrases with *an* sound like /æ/ + a word beginning with *n*. Practice saying the words. Draw a line to connect *an* to the vowel of the next word.

an architect	an economist	an interior designer	an office manager
an art teacher	an engineer	an interpreter	an optometrist

SPEAKING

A Make a list of facts you know about a famous person in your notebook.

B IN GROUPS Ask questions and guess who the famous person is. Use the Confident Communicator box to help you.

A: Is it a man or a woman? — *B: A …*
A: How old is he/she? — *B: I think he/she's about …*
A: When is his/her birthday? — *B: I don't know.*
A: Where's he/she from? — *B: He/She's from …*
A: Is he/she married? — *B: I think so. / I don't know.*
A: What does he/she do? — *B: He's/She's a/an …*
A: Is it … ? — *B: Yes, it is! / No, it isn't!*

CONFIDENT COMMUNICATOR
KEEP TALKING

If you don't know the answer to a question, say:
I don't know.
If you think you know an answer, but you are not sure, say:
I (don't) think so. / I think it's/she's/he's …

Family Connections

VOCABULARY family

A **Complete Sherry's family tree with words from the box.**

aunt brother cousin mother nephew niece son uncle

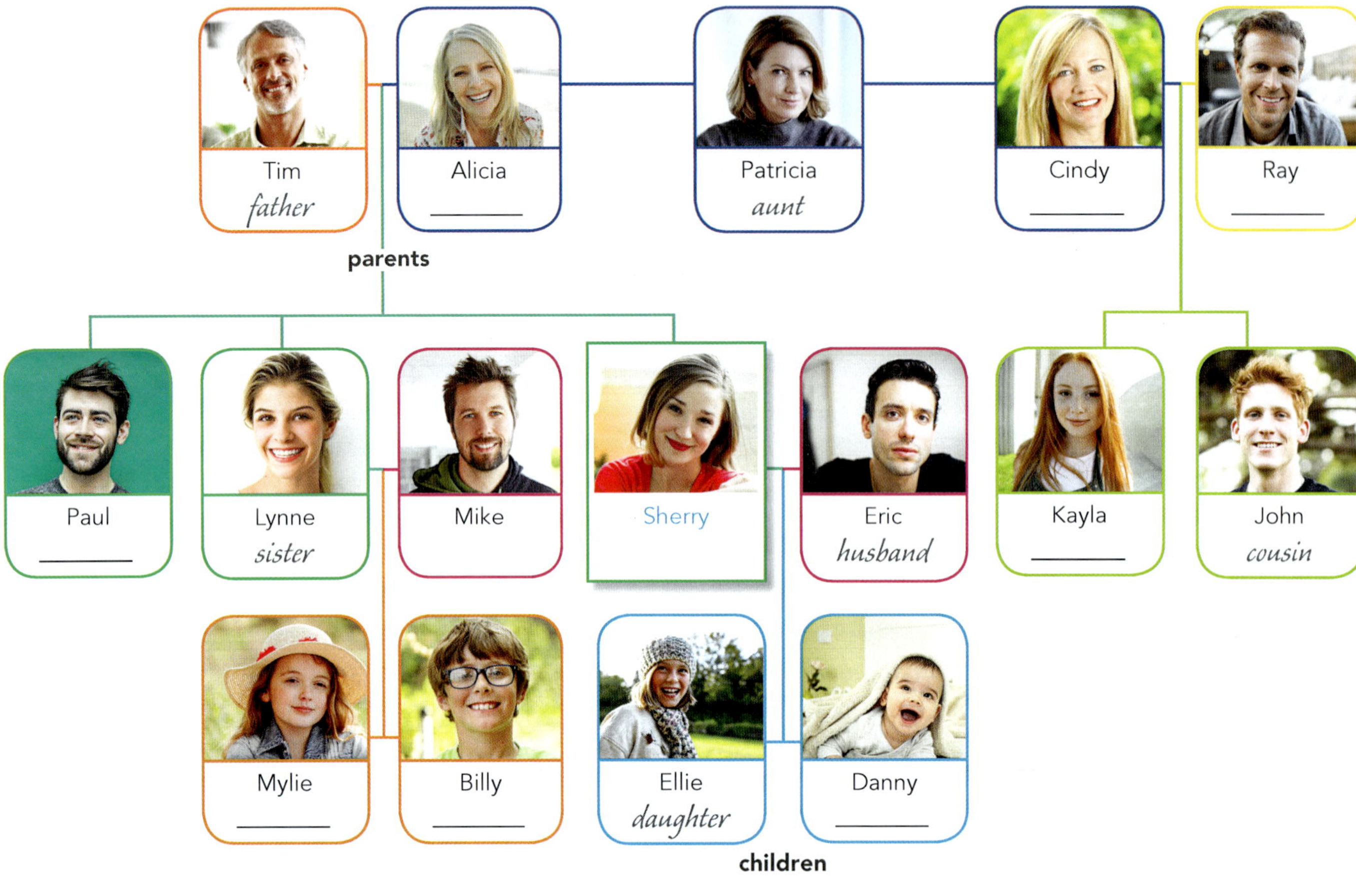

B **2.03 Listen and check your answers.**

MAKE IT REAL

People often use different words for immediate family members.

father: *dad, pa, pop, daddy* mother: *mom, mama, ma, mommy*

brother: *bro* sister: *sis*

GRAMMAR possessive adjectives and 's/s'

A **Read the examples. Then choose the correct option to complete the rules.**

Tim is **Sherry's** father.
Her **children's** names are Ellie and Danny.
Her **parents'** names are Tim and Alicia.
Whose sister is Sherry? She's Paul's and Lynne's sister.
Ellie and Danny are children. **Their** parents are Sherry and Eric.

Eric is married to **his** wife, Sherry.
Sherry has a sister. **Her** name is Lynne.

1. Show possession with *'s* for singular or irregular / plural nouns.
2. Show possession with *s'* for singular / plural nouns.
3. When you refer to a man, use the possessive adjective *his* / *her* / *their*.
4. When you refer to a woman, use the possessive adjective *his* / *her* / *their*.
5. When you refer to two or more people, use the possessive adjective *his* / *her* / *their*.
6. Use *Whose* / *Who* to ask how two people are connected in the family.

For more practice, go to page 144.

B **Find and correct one error in each sentence.**

Her ~~fathers~~ *father's* name is Tim.

1 Sherrys' mother's name is Alicia.

2 Her parent's hometown is Chicago.

3 Who's children are Danny and Ellie? They're Sherry's children.

4 Ray is Cindy's husband. Our children are Kayla and John.

5 Sherry's children's names' are Danny and Ellie.

C **IN PAIRS Ask each other questions about Sherry's family tree.**

A: Whose husband is Eric? *B: He's Sherry's husband.*

LISTENING

A **IN PAIRS Look at the family picture. Guess how the people are connected to Alan.**

B **2.04 LISTENING SKILL—Use visual clues Listen to Alan talk about the picture and complete.**

1 Mary is Alan's ___________.
2 Kaitlyn is Kevin's ___________.
3 Kevin is Alan's ___________. He's ___________ to Kaitlyn.
4 Linda is Alan's ___________. Her___________ is Steve.
5 Mindy is Alan's niece. Her___________ is Mary.
6 Robert isn't ___________. He's ___________ years old.

C **IN PAIRS THINKING SKILL—Analyze Discuss the questions.**

1 What is Sarah's relationship to Alan?
2 Does Sarah know Alan's family?
3 Why does Alan say, "Of course, Robert isn't married"?

SPEAKING

A **Draw your family tree in your notebook. Fill in some of the names, but leave the others blank.**

B **IN PAIRS Ask questions to complete your partner's family tree. Then look at your family tree and correct errors. Use the Confident Communicator box to help you.**

A: What's your aunt's name? *B: Her name is Anna. Her husband is Frank.*

CONFIDENT COMMUNICATOR
REPAIR IT

Names can be difficult to understand. Ask questions to check your understanding.
Can you repeat his/her name?
How do you spell that?

VOCABULARY jobs

A **IN GROUPS** Make a list of jobs you know in your notebook.

B Match the pictures to the jobs from the box. Write the words under each picture.

accountant	architect	computer technician	interpreter
journalist	nurse	pharmacist	pilot

1 
____

2 
____

3 
____

4 
____

5 
____

6 
____

7 
____

8 
____

LISTENING

A **LISTENING SKILL—Predict** Look at the family picture. What do you think Molly will talk about?

MAKE IT YOURS

Make a list of the jobs your family members have. Include your job or the job you want to have in the future. Use your dictionary if necessary.

B 2.05 Listen and answer the questions.

1 Who's in the picture? *Molly's aunt,* __________
2 Where are they? __________
3 How old is Jeff? __________
4 What is Jeff's job? __________
5 What is Elsa's job? __________
6 What is Pete's job? __________
7 How old is Laurie? __________

C **THINKING SKILL—Categorize** Discuss the questions.

1 What jobs in this lesson are associated with math ability, science ability, or creative ability?
2 What jobs require a university degree?

WRITING

A Complete the family profile using information from the table.

	Person 1	Person 2	Person 3	Person 4
Relationship to you	father	mother	uncle	sister
Age	65	58	60	25
Job	engineer	accountant	math teacher	manager
Place of work	retired	New Systems	Lincoln High School	a restaurant

MY PROFILE

MY FAMILY

The members of my family have interesting jobs. My dad is a/an **1** ______________, but he's **2** ______________ and he's retired now. My **3** ______________ is 58, and she's an accountant at **4** ______________. It's an IT company. My Uncle Joe is a **5** ______________ at Lincoln High School. He's my dad's brother. My sister is only **6** ______________, but she's the manager of a large restaurant.

B Complete the table for your family.

	Family Member 1: ______	Family Member 2: ______	Family Member 3: ______	Family Member 4: ______
Relationship to you				
Age				
Job				
Place of work				

C Write your family profile in your notebook.

D IN PAIRS Read and discuss your family profiles. Correct grammar, spelling, and punctuation.

SPEAKING

A Prepare to talk about your favorite family picture and make notes in your notebook. Use the Confident Communicator box to help you.

1. Who's in the picture and what is their relationship to you?
2. Where are the people in the picture?
3. What are their relationships to other family members (for example, *my mother's sister*)?
4. How old are they?
5. What do they do?

CONFIDENT COMMUNICATOR

KEEP TALKING

When you use notes to help you talk about something, look quickly at your notes, but don't read them aloud.

B IN GROUPS Share and discuss your picture.

My favorite picture is of me, my sister, and our cousins Ronny and Jenny. Ronny is a computer programmer. Jenny is …

Language and Life

Self-awareness – The Right Job

A 2.06 **Read the Careers Profile and the job ads, then answer the question in your notebook.**

Which two jobs fit David's interests and abilities?

CAREERS PROFILE | **Name:** David Monetti

For each category, choose two areas that describe your interests and abilities.

Personality	☐ organized	■ friendly	☐ patient	■ independent
Natural abilities	■ verbal	■ logical/ mathematical	☐ creative	☐ social
Academic skills	☐ science and math	■ language	■ technology	☐ arts

CAREERS PROFILE Results

High school English teacher

Job description: Teach grammar, writing, and literature. Patience, good communication skills, and IT/social media skills are necessary.

Journalist for city newspaper

Job description: Talk to people and write stories. Need good English and computer skills. We want a creative, independent person.

Computer technician for large company

Job description: Work with computers and help people with computer problems. Lots of travel. A science and engineering education is required.

Marketer for small communications company

Job description: Need a friendly, creative, social person. Good computer and social media skills are necessary. Art or design education is not necessary, but good writing is very important.

B **IN PAIRS** **Compare your ideas and discuss.**

A: I think the right jobs for David are English teacher and journalist. His verbal and language skills are good.
B: Maybe journalist, but not English teacher. He isn't patient.

C **IN GROUPS** **Complete with the kind of personality, abilities, and skills you need for each job.**

1 accountant: *organized,* ________________
2 nurse: ________________
3 journalist: ________________
4 engineer: ________________
5 designer: ________________

D **Complete a Careers Profile for you.**

CAREERS PROFILE	**Name:**			
For each category, choose two areas that describe your interests and abilities.				
Personality	☐ organized	☐ friendly	☐ patient	☐ independent
Natural abilities	☐ verbal	☐ logical/ mathematical	☐ creative	☐ social
Academic skills	☐ science and math	☐ language	☐ technology	☐ arts

E **Complete a list of jobs and skills for you.**

Possible jobs

Job:

Skills I have for the job:

Job:

Skills I have for the job:

Job:

Skills I have for the job:

F **IN GROUPS** **Share your lists of jobs and skills. Discuss and make suggestions.**

A: What about an architect? Your logic and math skills are good, and you're creative.
B: Or a math teacher. You're patient.

MAKE IT DIGITAL

Go online and look for job listings in your area. Think about which jobs are good for you, based on your interests and abilities.

VOCABULARY review

SCORE: / 10

A Choose the correct option to complete the sentences about Elena's family.

My **1 mother / father** is very creative. She's an art **2 engineer / teacher**. My mother's sister Ana is my **3 aunt / cousin**. Her house is beautiful. She's an **4 accountant / interior designer**. Nina is Ana's daughter. She's my **5 sister / cousin**. When I have a laptop problem, I call her. She's a **6 computer technician / marketer**. My **7 father / daughter** works for a large company. His name is Ricardo. He speaks English and Portuguese. He's an **8 interpreter / office manager**. My **9 grandfather / uncle** is my father's father. He sells computers. He's a small business **10 owner / optometrist**.

GRAMMAR review

SCORE: / 10

A Complete the job ad with *a*, *an*, or X (no article).

Do you want **1** _____ interesting job? Think about a job as **2** _____ social media manager. **3** _____ social media manager writes **4** _____ comments and connects with **5** _____ customers. Contact us at our website to apply.

B Complete the sentences with words from the box.

's s' his her their

1 My parent ____________ names are Mark and Cindy.
2 My sister is named Kathy, but ____________ nickname is Kat.
3 My brother ____________ name is Jeff.
4 He's married to ____________ wife, Ann.
5 ____________ daughter's name is Barbara.

16–20 correct: You can talk about family and jobs. You can use *a*/*an* and the verb *be*.
0–15 correct: Look again at the Vocabulary and Grammar sections in the unit.

TOTAL SCORE: / 20

WHAT DO YOU KNOW NOW? Look back at page 17 and add the words you know now to the boxes.

FOLLOW A PRO INFORMATION TECHNOLOGY (IT)

Take the quiz about IT (information technology). Go to Follow A Pro on page 128 to find the answers. Then learn more about the IT industry.

1 Which country has the most internet users?
a China **b** the UK **c** the US

2 How many new viruses go into the internet every month?
a 360 **b** 6,000 **c** 10,000

3 Why is November 30 a special day? It's …
a clean your computer day. **b** internet safety day. **c** computer security day.

4 What percentage of internet traffic is web robots?
a 8% **b** 55% **c** 21%

UNIT 3 Fun and Games

WHAT DO YOU ALREADY KNOW?

1 **Think of words you know about free-time activities. Write activities that you can do indoors and outdoors.**

2 **IN PAIRS Share and compare your activities. Add more words to your lists.**

Outdoor activities

play tennis

Indoor activities

play music

VIDEO

DISCUSS & SHARE

3 **IN GROUPS Watch the video and answer the question.**

SYM How much time do you need alone or with other people?

In this unit, you will ...

- express likes and dislikes, recommend free-time activities, and talk about an event.
- use thinking skills: categorize, infer, and recall.
- read a magazine interview.
- use strategies to keep talking and emphasize preferences, giving reasons, and expressing rules.
- use creativity skills to work with others and create an interest group for a website.
- learn tips for a successful oral presentation.

Like It, Love It, or Hate It?

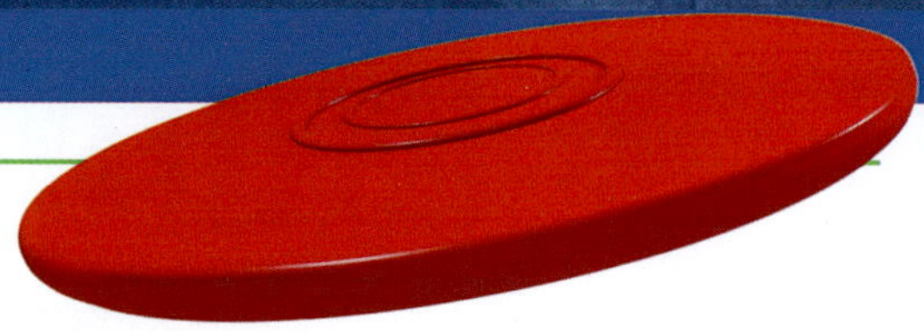

READING

A **IN GROUPS** Discuss free-time activities. What do you like doing in your free time? Which type of activity is the most popular in your group?

B **3.01 READING SKILL—Infer** Read the magazine interview and answer the question. Who is Otto?

NEW FRISBEE CHAMPIONS!

Here is an interview with Chris Watson, one half of the Chris-Otto Frisbee team. Chris and Otto are this year's winners.

Interviewer: Congratulations, Chris! You and Otto are the winners! Do you have time to talk to me?

Chris: Sure, thanks. Otto is a great Frisbee player! He runs really fast, and he always catches the Frisbee. Otto loves Frisbee, too. We practice together every day.

Interviewer: Does he like other outdoor activities?

Chris: Well, yes, he likes hiking, but he doesn't like hiking in cold weather.

Interviewer: Does he have any special likes or dislikes?

Chris: Yes, he does. He loves watching TV. He watches soccer and football with me a lot. I like golf, but Otto thinks it's boring. I don't watch it often. And … let's see. He likes eating—a lot! And he hates cats!

Interviewer: Thanks, Chris. Good luck to you and Otto next season.

Chris: Thanks.

Otto: Woof!

C **THINKING SKILL—Categorize** Read the interview again and write Otto's likes and dislikes in the table.

Otto likes …	Otto doesn't like …

VOCABULARY

A Read the verbs and complete the sentences for you. Discuss with a partner.

1 I ______________ sports.
2 I ______________ romantic movies.
3 I ______________ hiking.
4 I ______________ playing video games.
5 I ______________ using social media.
6 I ______________ listening to music.

GRAMMAR simple present statements and *yes/no* questions

A Read the examples from the interview. Then choose the correct option to complete the rules.

He loves watching sports on TV.	He doesn't like hiking in cold weather.
I like golf.	Do you have time to talk to me? Yes, I do.
I don't watch it often.	Does he have any special likes or dislikes? Yes, he does.

1. For statements with *I*, *you*, *we*, and *they*, **add** / **don't add** an *–s* to the verb.
2. For statements with *he*, *she*, and *it*, **add** / **don't add** an *–s* to the verb.
3. The correct word order for *yes/no* questions is **Do or Does + subject + verb** / **Subject + do or does + verb**.
4. Short answers to *yes/no* questions end in **do or does** / **a verb**.

For more practice, go to page 145.

B Choose the correct option.

1. **Do** / **Does** you like soccer? **Yes, I like.** / **Yes, I do.**
2. I **love** / **loves** tennis, but my brother **isn't** / **doesn't** like it.
3. **Do** / **Does** your dad like watching sports on TV? No, he **don't** / **doesn't**.
4. My sister and I **love** / **loves** video games, but my brother doesn't **like** / **likes** them.
5. He **play** / **plays** games on his phone, but I **think** / **thinks** games are boring.

MAKE IT REAL

Alternative phrases for short answers:
A: Do you like swimming?
B: Not really. / No, but I like … / It's OK. / Sure. / Of course.

C IN PAIRS Discuss preferences.

A: Do you like basketball? *B: I like watching it, but I don't like playing it.*
A: Do you like playing soccer? *B: Yes, I do. I like watching it, too!*

PRONUNCIATION third person –s

A 3.02 Listen and notice the final sound of each word. Practice saying the words.

Sounds like /s/: likes, hates, walks, thinks
Sounds like /z/: loves, swims, plays, runs
Sounds like /iz/: watches, uses, practices, catches

B IN PAIRS Practice reading aloud. Pronounce the verbs correctly.

1. Otto runs fast, and he always catches the Frisbee.
2. My brother loves tennis. He practices every day.
3. My sister thinks hiking is boring, but she likes swimming.
4. My dad hates social media, but he uses it for his business.

SPEAKING

A Make a list of free-time activities that you like in your notebook.

B IN PAIRS Discuss what you like and don't like. Draw faces next to the activities on your list according to your partner's answers.

A: Do you like playing video games? *B: No, I hate it!*

C IN GROUPS Find another pair. Tell them about your partner's preferences. Use the Confident Communicator box to help you.

Mark hates playing video games, but he likes playing cards.

CONFIDENT COMMUNICATOR
KEEP TALKING

Add words to give more information about your preferences.
*I **really** like/hate swimming.*
*I don't like swimming **very much**.*
*I like swimming **a lot**.*

LESSON 2 Preferences

VOCABULARY free-time activities

A Complete the table with words from the box.

audiobooks	dancing	movies	music	online videos	parties	podcasts
shopping	soccer	to eat	TV	video games	with friends	~~the movies~~

listen to	watch	play	go	go to	go out
podcasts	*movies*			*the movies*	

B IN GROUPS Discuss whether you like or don't like the same things.

A: Do you like listening to music or to podcasts? I prefer music.
B: Music.
C: Music.
D: Podcasts.
A: OK, three for music and one for podcasts.

MAKE IT YOURS

List other free-time activities that you like to do or places that you like to go to.

LISTENING

A As a class, list some of your favorite games, movies, musicians, and TV shows.

games ______________________________

movies ______________________________

musicians ______________________________

TV shows ______________________________

B 3.03 Listen to the phone conversation and answer the question. What is the event?

C 3.03 LISTENING SKILL—Take notes Listen again and complete the notes.

Event:

Date:

Time:

Place:

Ticket price:

D 3.03 THINKING SKILL—Understand Listen again and choose the correct option.

1 Who buys the tickets?
a Rob **b** Sandy **c** Rob and Sandy

2 Who pays for the tickets?
a Rob **b** Sandy **c** Rob and Sandy

GRAMMAR the imperative

A Read the examples from the conversation and choose the correct option to complete the rules.

Listen to this!
Please get me a ticket!
Don't forget to write down the information.
Tell me the date again, please.

1. We use the imperative to …
   a give opinions. **b** give orders or instructions. **c** talk about likes and dislikes.
2. The verb form in imperative sentences is …
   a base form. **b** *to* + verb. **c** verb + *–ing*.
3. To form a negative imperative, use …
   a verb + *not*. **b** *doesn't* + verb. **c** *don't* + verb.
4. For a polite imperative, add *please* … of the sentence.
   a at the beginning **b** at the end **c** at the beginning or end

For more practice, go to page 146.

B Complete the conversation with verbs from the box.

don't | buy forget listen tell turn use

Erika: **1** ____________ to this new song by Logan Williams.
Laura: It's great! **2** ____________ up the volume!
Erika: Here. **3** ____________ my headphones.
Laura: Excellent! What's the name of the song?
Erika: "Party Night." The song is great, but **4** ____________ the album. The other songs aren't very good.
Laura: OK. Hey, **5** ____________ to get that new app. It's really good.
Erika: Oh, yeah. **6** ____________ me the name again, please.
Laura: It's called *Guess Who*.

C IN PAIRS Role-play the conversation in B with a singer, song, and app that you like.

SPEAKING

A Complete the table with things you like and don't like. Add two more things to the list of activities.

Activities	Like	Don't Like
Movies		
Apps		
Books		
TV shows		

B IN GROUPS Give recommendations. Use the Confident Communicator box to help you.

CONFIDENT COMMUNICATOR
KEEP TALKING

When you give a negative recommendation, try to give a reason.
OK, for movies, go see the new Spielberg movie. It's excellent.
Don't see Mystery on the Beach. It's terrible/boring/silly/violent.

LESSON 3

Special Events

LISTENING

A Think about the words in the box and discuss the questions.

concerts festivals sports events other types of competitions

1 Which special events happen in your area?
2 What type of event is your favorite?

B 3.04 LISTENING SKILL—Listen for gist Listen and choose the correct option.

1 What type of recording is this?
a a TV program b an advertisement c a podcast
2 What is the speaker talking about?
a a festival b a concert c a race

C 3.04 Listen again and choose *True* or *False*.

1 This is a national festival. True / False
2 The festival includes two races. True / False
3 The soccer players are children. True / False
4 The festival is open eight hours every day. True / False
5 The festival doesn't welcome pets. True / False
6 Buy your tickets at the festival to get a discount. True / False

D THINKING SKILL—Recall Write and compare.

1 Make a list of the events from the advertisement. With a partner, compare your lists and add to them.

VOCABULARY special events

A Write two words from the box in each column.

baseball motorcycle pop photography hip hop singing horse soccer

a … concert	a … game	a … race	a … competition
rock	football	10-km	cooking
classical	basketball	bicycle	dance

B Complete the sentences for you.

1 I love ______________ concerts.
2 I think ______________ races are dangerous.
3 I don't like ______________ competitions.
4 I love to watch ______________ games.
5 I like going to ______________ festivals.

MAKE IT YOURS

What types of local or special events are in your area? Add more events to the lists in **A**.

C IN GROUPS Discuss your opinions.

A: I love rock concerts.
B: Me, too.
C: I prefer pop concerts.

WRITING

A Read the poster and label with words from the box.

date	description of event	name of event	place
a recommendation	ticket information	time	rules

1 ____________
2 ____________
3 ____________
4 ____________
5 ____________
6 ____________
7 ____________
8 ____________

B **IN GROUPS** Plan a poster for an event in your area.

EVENT PLANNING FORM

Name and/or type of event ____________
Specific information about the event ____________
Place ____________
Date ____________
Starting/Ending times ____________
Ticket information ____________
Rules ____________
Recommendation ____________
Other information ____________

C Create your poster. Emphasize important information and make your poster attractive.

SPEAKING

A **IN GROUPS** Describe the event from your poster. Use the Confident Communicator box to help you.

A: The event is … *B: The rules are …*

A: It's in/near … *B: My favorite thing is … / I don't recommend the …*

B Share with the class. Show your poster and describe the event.

C Take a class vote. What poster do you like best? What event do you want to go to?

CONFIDENT COMMUNICATOR
KEEP TALKING

Ways to express rules:

No dogs/food/backpacks *Children over 12 only*
Pets/food/drinks are OK *Drinks only; no food*

Language and Life

Creativity – An Interest Group

A 3.05 **Read the social media web page. Then choose the correct option below.**

GET TOGETHER

Name of group: Music Lovers join

Do you love music? Do you sing or play an instrument? This is the group for you! We like to go to concerts together, but we LOVE to make our own music!

Name of group: Latinos Play join

We are a group of students from Latin American countries. We like eating food from our countries and meeting other Latin American students here in Los Angeles. If you speak Spanish and love good food, join our group!

Upcoming Meetings

Attend	Attend	Attend
15 SEP — Sat. Sep 15, 7... Music Lovers, Thompson Park	15 SEP — Sat. Sep 15, 9... Latinos Play Public library	16 SEP — Sun. Sep 16, 8... Biking Club, Riverside Park
15 going	8 going	12 going

How to join Get Together

Register for free. Then click on your interests and read about local groups. The members of the groups meet and do different activities. Join the groups that interest you.

How to create a Get Together group

You can start your own Get Together group. Click on "Create a Group." Enter your location. Click on your interest for the new group. Choose a title for the group. Write a short profile of the group. Click "Create Group."

CREATE A GROUP

1 People use this website to …
   a take classes to learn new hobbies. **b** meet new friends with similar interests. **c** meet people to date.
2 The members of the first group like to …
   a listen to music. **b** play music. **c** listen to and play music.
3 The members of the second group are all from …
   a Latin America. **b** Los Angeles. **c** the same country.

B IN PAIRS **Read the social media post. Then discuss.**

1 What is Miguel's problem?
2 Are either of the two groups in **A** right for him?

Language Institute Blog

miguel Posted SEP 17 7:06 p.m.
My name is Miguel, and I'm from Ecuador. I study English in a language institute in Los Angeles. I want to meet new friends with similar interests and practice my English. I like hiking, concerts, and good food. My favorite foods are Italian and Chinese food. Please give me some ideas.

follow

C **IN PAIRS** Choose Miguel's interests to help him create a new Get Together group.

GET TOGETHER

NEW GROUP

Location: Los Angeles, CA

Interests

watching sports ♡ | playing team sports ♡ | hiking ♡ | dancing ♡ | biking ♡

dating ♡ | pets ♡ | food & restaurants ♡ | cooking ♡ | international students ♡

concerts ♡ | musicians ♡ | movies ♡ | theater ♡ | gaming ♡

D Choose one of Miguel's interests from C and create a new group.

GET TOGETHER

NEW GROUP

Location: Los Angeles, CA

Interests

Interest area:

Name of group:

Description of group:

E Take a class vote. Read your description of Miguel's interest group and decide which new interest group is best for him.

F **IN GROUPS** Discuss.

1. Do you know of any websites like Get Together in your area?
2. Do you use a website like Get Together? If so, what groups do you belong to?
3. What are your interests? Do you want to join a website like Get Together?

MAKE IT DIGITAL

Start a network of interest groups in your school or institute to meet people with similar interests and practice your English.

VOCABULARY review

SCORE: / 10

A Match the sentence beginning (1–10) to the sentence end (a–j). Write the letter.

1 Dani likes to read books and listen to ____
2 Sally loves to dance and go to ____
3 Erik likes to watch ____
4 Hannah loves to play ____
5 Rich loves to go ____
6 Pedro likes to go out ____
7 Yumiko likes to run and play ____
8 Marta likes to go for ____
9 Isobel and her friends love to use ____
10 My dog hates to take ____

a games on her phone.
b shopping and spend money.
c audiobooks.
d parties with friends.
e movies at home on his big TV.
f a bath.
g walks in the park.
h social media.
i tennis.
j to eat in restaurants.

GRAMMAR review

SCORE: / 10

A Choose the correct option.

Berta: Hi, Frida! I'm in the online Music Interest Group with you. **1** Do you play / Do you plays more than one musical instrument?

Frida: Yes, I **2** am / do. Drums and piano! I **3** practice / practices every day. My parents **4** don't like / doesn't like the drums! I'm in the school band. **5** Does your school have / Do your school have a band?

Berta: No, it **6** doesn't / don't. But there's a music and dance club.

Frida: **7** Do you dance / Does you dance well?

Berta: No, I **8** don't / doesn't. Oh, I have to go to class!

Frida: OK. Please **9** Text / text again soon. **10** Not forget / Don't forget to post a picture! Here's a picture of me!

16–20 correct: You can talk about likes, dislikes, and free-time activities. You can use the simple present and *yes/no* questions.
0–15 correct: Look again at the Vocabulary and Grammar sections in the unit.

TOTAL SCORE: / 20

WHAT DO YOU KNOW NOW? Look back at page 27 and add the words you know now to the boxes.

STUDY SKILLS ORAL PRESENTATIONS

Take the quiz about oral presentations. Go to **Study Skills** on page 129 to find the answers. Then learn more about oral presentations.

1 You need to spend 50% of your time writing your presentation.
a true **b** false

2 When people see pictures, they remember … of what they hear and see.
a 60% **b** 80% **c** 95%

3 You want to begin your talk. What do you say?
a "Please listen to me." **b** "Silence!" **c** "Hello. Today I'm talking about …"

4 You want to finish your talk. What do you say?
a "That's all." **b** "Thank you for listening. Any questions?" **c** "The end!"

UNIT 4 That's Life!

WHAT DO YOU ALREADY KNOW?

1 **Think of words about the activities you do every day. Write the words for the activities.**

2 **IN PAIRS** **Share and compare your information. Add more words to your lists.**

Planned Activities

eat breakfast

Unexpected Things

get sick

VIDEO

DISCUSS & SHARE

3 **IN GROUPS** **Watch the video and answer the question.**

SYM Do you plan your day or decide what to do at the last minute?

In this unit, you will ...

- talk about daily activities and how often you do them. Describe a day off.
- use thinking skills: draw conclusions, summarize, and recall.
- read about a reporter's typical day.
- use strategies to start and keep talking by giving examples and expressing frequency.
- use adaptability skills to give advice about keeping life interesting.
- follow an emergency worker to learn about this job and the skills needed for this industry.

LESSON 1 **A Day in the Life**

READING

A Take a class survey. How many people think their lives are boring, average, or exciting?

B 4.01 **THINKING SKILL—Analyze** Read the blog post. In your opinion, is Jerry's life boring, average, or exciting?

The Daily Blog

Jan 21 1:43 p.m.

A Day in the Life of a Reporter

I'm a reporter. I work for an entertainment magazine in New York City. My friends think my job is amazing because I meet famous people. But this is my typical day.

I get up at about 6:30 a.m., and then I **walk my dog**, **have coffee**, and **get ready for work**. I leave home at 7:15 a.m., and I **take the subway** to my office. I **start work** at 8:00 a.m. I don't eat breakfast at home because I don't have time. I buy something at the café in the subway station. At work, I go to meetings and write articles for the magazine. I also **make** a lot of **phone calls** to get interviews with people. The interviews are interesting, but sometimes the people I interview aren't very friendly or they don't have time to talk.

In the evening, I **go home** and walk my dog again. Then, I **have dinner** and watch TV for about two hours. I go to bed at about 10:00 p.m. On weekends, I go out with friends, go shopping, or go to a movie.

follow

C **IN PAIRS READING SKILL—Scan** Find the answers as quickly as possible.

1 What time does Jerry get up?
2 Where does he live?
3 Why do his friends think his job is amazing?
4 How does he get to work?
5 Who does he go out with on weekends?

VOCABULARY

A Find words from the blog post that match the definitions. Write the word.

1 begin your workday: ____________
2 exercise with your dog: ____________
3 drink coffee: ____________
4 prepare for work: ____________
5 travel by subway: ____________
6 call people: ____________
7 return to your home: ____________
8 eat dinner: ____________

GRAMMAR simple present information questions

A Complete the questions with words from the box.

how what when where who why

Information Questions: Question Word + *Do/Does* + Subject + Verb / Verb Phrase

1 ____________ do your parents do?	They're teachers.
2 ____________ does your brother work?	He works at a bank.
3 ____________ does he work?	He works from Monday to Friday.
4 ____________ do you like your job?	I like it because it's very interesting.
5 ____________ do you get to work?	I take the bus.
6 ____________ do you see on weekends?	I see my best friend.

For more practice, go to page 146.

B Unscramble the questions.

1 do / on weekends / you / what / do / ?

2 in your free time / who / you / do / see / ?

3 go / you / where / on vacation / do / ?

4 English / you / study / do / why / ?

5 do / when / you / your English homework / do / ?

6 to English class / you / do / get / how / ?

C IN PAIRS Ask and answer the questions in B.

PRONUNCIATION word stress in information questions

A 4.02 Listen and underline the stressed words.

1 What do you do?
2 Where do you live?
3 Why do you like your job?
4 When do you go on vacation?
5 How do you get to class?

B 4.02 Listen again. Practice reading the questions with the correct word stress.

SPEAKING

A Use the cues to write interview questions.

1 What / do?

2 Where / work or study?

3 When / have English class?

4 How / get to work?

5 What time / start work?

6 What / do in your free time?

B IN PAIRS Interview your partner. Write his/her answers in A.

C IN GROUPS Is your life boring, average, or exciting? Are your partners' lives exciting? Use the Confident Communicator box to help you.

CONFIDENT COMMUNICATOR
START TALKING

To describe your life, give examples to support your opinion using *because*.
My life is exciting because I travel a lot / meet a lot of interesting people / have a great social life.
My life is average because I like my job, but it isn't exciting / I just do normal things.
My life is boring because my job isn't interesting / I don't do many interesting things / I do the same things every day.

LESSON 2 Always? Sometimes? Never?

LISTENING

A As a class, discuss jobs you think are exciting.

B 4.03 Listen to an interview with an actress. Does she think her life is exciting? Why or why not?

MAKE IT REAL

Really means *very*: *That's really early.*
Some Americans say *real* for *really*: *That's real early.*
Kind of means *a little*: *My job is kind of unusual.*
Americans often pronounce it as *kinda*.

C 4.03 **LISTENING SKILL—Listen for specific information** Listen again and choose the correct option.

1 Audrey often starts work …
a at 6:00. **b** at 8:00. **c** at 10:00.
2 She frequently finishes work at …
a six o'clock in the evening. **b** seven thirty in the evening. **c** eight or nine at night.
3 On weekends, Audrey almost always …
a works. **b** spends time with her family. **c** goes to San Francisco.
4 Audrey and her family go to San Francisco to …
a see her parents. **b** go to the zoo. **c** work.
5 Audrey thinks that her life is …
a exciting. **b** normal. **c** boring.

D **IN PAIRS THINKING SKILL—Summarize** Describe Audrey's life.

A: She's married / an actress.
B: She has children / an interesting life / a difficult job.
A: She works from … to …
B: On weekdays / weekends / Saturdays / Sundays, she …
A: She doesn't often …

VOCABULARY frequency and time expressions

A Complete the table with the words in the box.

3:00, a day, a week, week, day, Friday, March, year, March 20, month, morning, ~~2020~~, night, once, the evening, three times, Tuesdays, twice

in	on	at	every	several times	… a day / month / year
2020					

B IN PAIRS Ask and answer questions. Use frequency expressions.

1 How often do you eat at restaurants?
2 How often does your family go on vacation?
3 How often do you play video games?
4 How often do you have English class?
5 How often do you go shopping?

GRAMMAR frequency adverbs

A Look at the scale. Then complete the rules.

100%	75%	50%	25%	10%	0%
always	usually	often	sometimes	rarely	never

I'm always tired!
We usually work a lot of hours.
Sometimes we go to San Francisco to see my parents.
I rarely work on Saturdays.

1 Frequency adverbs come **before** / **after** the verb *be*.
2 Frequency adverbs come **before** / **after** other verbs.
3 Frequency or time expressions come **at the end** / **at the beginning or end** of a sentence.

For more practice, go to page 147.

B Look at the scale. Then complete the sentences.

100%	75%	50%	25%	10%	0%
eats breakfast	sees friends on the weekend	listens to podcasts	talks on the phone	is sad	is late to work

1 Robert ____________ talks on the phone. (25%)
2 He ______________________________
3 ______________________________
4 ______________________________
5 ______________________________
6 ______________________________

SPEAKING

A Complete the survey for you.

How often do you ...	You			
go out to eat?				
go to a movie?				
take a vacation?				
use social media?				

B IN GROUPS Write each group member's name at the top of the table in A. Ask and answer the questions for each group member. Use the Confident Communicator box to help you. Then discuss. Do the people in your group have similar routines or very different routines?

CONFIDENT COMMUNICATOR
KEEP TALKING

When you don't know the exact frequency of an activity, use words like *about*, *around*, and *more or less*: *about once a month*, *around four times a year*, *more or less twice a day*.

The Perfect Day

VOCABULARY routine activities

A Match the expressions from the box to the photos.

cook	do housework	get dressed	go to the gym
go out with friends	hang out at home	take a nap	take a shower

1  ______

2  ______

3  ______

4  ______

5  ______

6  ______

7  ______

8  ______

B **IN PAIRS** Discuss the activities using frequency expressions.

A: I often do housework. *B: I never take a nap.*

A: I rarely cook. *B: I usually go to the gym in the morning.*

LISTENING

a 

b 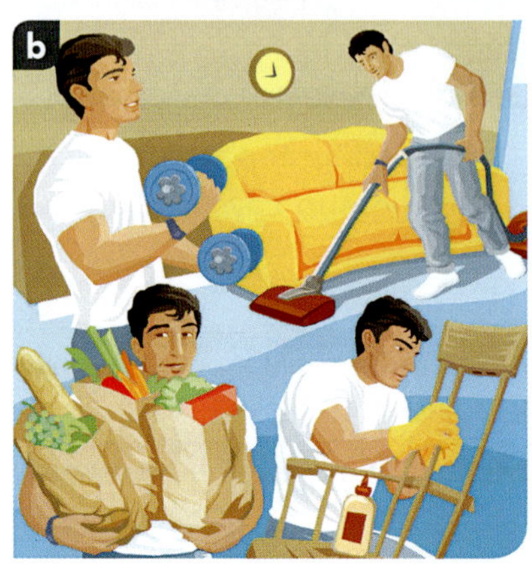

A Look at the pictures. Which type of day off do you prefer?

B 4.04 **LISTENING SKILL—Listen for gist** Listen to a radio show. Write *C* (*crazy*) or *L* (*lazy*) for each caller.

1 Brendon: ______ 3 Ali: ______

2 Carla: ______ 4 Melissa: ______

C 4.04 **IN PAIRS THINKING SKILL—Recall** Listen again. List the activities each caller does on a day off.

1 Brendon: gets up late, ______

2 Carla: takes a shower, ______

3 Ali: goes to the gym, ______

4 Melissa: hangs out at home, ______

D **IN PAIRS** Compare your lists with another partner.

MAKE IT YOURS

Make a list of activities that you like doing on a day off.

WRITING

A Read the blog post. In your opinion, is Olivia's day crazy or lazy? Discuss.

THE PERFECT DAY OFF

March 2 3:32 p.m.

I love to write this blog, but I also love to have a day off! On my perfect day off, I usually get up late. I take a shower and get dressed. I go out and eat a big breakfast. After breakfast, I go for a walk. Then, I usually hang out with friends. We go to a café or go shopping. Sometimes we go to a movie. In the evening, I almost always order food, usually pizza. I don't like cooking! I never read blogs or use social media on my day off.

follow

B Complete the table for you.

	Activities on a Day Off
always	
usually	
often	
sometimes	
rarely	
never	

C Write a paragraph about your perfect day off in your notebook.

D **IN PAIRS** Read your partner's paragraph. Answer the questions and make recommendations. Use your partner's comments to make any changes to your paragraph.

1 Does your partner …

- **a** capitalize words correctly? Yes / No
- **b** use *be* correctly? Yes / No
- **c** have any spelling errors? Yes / No
- **d** have any grammar errors? Yes / No

SPEAKING

A **IN GROUPS** Discuss your perfect day off. As you listen to each person, write *C* (*crazy*) or *L* (*lazy*), depending on the person's favorite type of day off.

B Take a class survey to see how many people enjoy lazy days and how many enjoy crazy days. Use the Confident Communicator box to help you.

CONFIDENT COMMUNICATOR
KEEP TALKING

You can use negative verbs with *always*, *usually*, *often*, and *sometimes*. Notice the word order:
I don't always eat breakfast.
I don't usually exercise on Saturdays.
I don't often get up late.
I sometimes don't check my email.

Language and Life

Adaptability – An Interesting Life

A 4.05 **Read the social media web page. In your opinion, why is Andy bored? Discuss. Do your classmates agree?**

I Need Advice!

Andy6_24:

I'm 25, and I live in Tampa, Florida, with my two friends Joe and Mario. I have a good job. I'm a nurse, and I work at a big hospital. My work schedule is 9:00 to 5:00 Monday through Friday. I eat lunch in the hospital cafeteria at 1:00 p.m. every day. I always go to the gym after work. In the evening, my roommates and I cook dinner—usually pasta or burgers. We watch TV for about two hours, and I almost always go to bed at about 10:30 p.m. On Saturdays, I go to the gym in the morning and go shopping or do housework in the afternoon. On Saturday evenings, my roommates and I usually order pizza and watch movies. On Sundays, I always play soccer with my friends in the afternoon. I have a very good life—nice friends and a good job, but I'm kind of bored. What do you recommend?

B Complete the notes with information from the web page.

Weekdays:

9:00–5:00 *works at the hospital*
1:00 p.m.
after work
in the evening

Saturdays:
in the morning
in the afternoon
in the evening

Sundays:
in the afternoon

C IN PAIRS Write recommendations to Andy for making his life more interesting.

I Need Advice!

Hi, Andy. We have some suggestions. Don't always watch TV after dinner. Go out and ... Don't ... every day.

D IN GROUPS Think of more recommendations for Andy to make his life more interesting.

E IN GROUPS Discuss your routine. Give each other recommendations to make your lives more exciting.

MAKE IT DIGITAL

Post ideas for people to make their lives more interesting on your own social media site.

VOCABULARY review

SCORE: / 10

A Complete the sentences with verbs from the box.

exercise	go	get	get up	~~hang out~~
have	order	start	take	walk

I'm a dessert blogger, and I have a usual daily routine. I **1** ____________ at 9:00, **2** ____________ coffee, and **3** ____________ the dog. Then, I **4** ____________ a shower and **5** ____________ ready for my workday. I **6** ____________ work at 11:30. I eat lunch at a different restaurant every day. After lunch, I **7** ____________ a dessert from the menu to eat. In the afternoon, I write my blog. Sunday is my day off. I don't just **8** ____________ at home. After all those desserts, I **9** ____________ to the gym and **10** ____________ for an hour!

GRAMMAR review

SCORE: / 10

A Write the question that asks about the underlined information.

1 I talk to <u>my friends</u> several times a day. ____________
2 We do <u>housework</u> on Sundays. ____________
3 My sister works <u>in a café</u> on weekends. ____________
4 I eat <u>cake</u> every afternoon. ____________
5 He studies English <u>because it's fun</u>! ____________

B Rewrite the sentences with the words in parentheses.

1 Meg takes a nap in the afternoon. (often) ____________
2 Mr. Nelson is late for class. (never) ____________
3 Kyle sees his parents. (twice a year) ____________
4 Anita takes the train to work. (rarely) ____________
5 We're at the gym on Sundays. (always) ____________

16–20 correct: You can talk about daily activities and frequency. You can use simple present information questions and frequency adverbs.
0–15 correct: Look again at the Vocabulary and Grammar sections in the unit.

TOTAL SCORE: / 20

WHAT DO YOU KNOW NOW? Look back at page 37 and add the words you know now to the boxes.

FOLLOW A PRO EMERGENCY SERVICES

Take the quiz about emergency services. Go to Follow A Pro on page 130 to find the answers. Then learn more about the emergency services industry.

1 The oldest emergency telephone number is 999. How old is it?
a over 70 years old **b** over 80 years old **c** over 90 years old

2 How many hours of training do you need to become a paramedic?
a about 2,000 **b** about 1,000 **c** about 500

3 What US state has a festival every year to celebrate its emergency workers?
a Washington **b** California **c** Alabama

4 70% of emergency medical technicians in the US are male.
a true **b** false

UNIT 5

Finding Your Way

WHAT DO YOU ALREADY KNOW?

1 Think of places you usually go and places you sometimes go. Write the names of the places.

2 **IN PAIRS** Share and compare your information. Add more words to your list.

Places I usually go

school

Places I sometimes go

museum

VIDEO

DISCUSS & SHARE

3 **IN GROUPS** **Watch the video and answer the question.**

SYM Do you ask for directions or try to find your way?

In this unit, you will ...

- talk about places to live, your neighborhood, and directions.
- use thinking skills: apply, evaluate, and analyze.
- read about unusual places to live.
- use strategies to keep talking by making guesses.
- use problem-solving skills to create a guide to your neighborhood.
- learn research skills for school and work.

READING

A **Look at the pictures in B and discuss the questions. Do you want to live somewhere like this? Why or why not?**

B **5.01 READING SKILL—Scan for specific information** **Read the article and answer the questions.**

PLACES WE LIVE

For many young people, the idea of buying a **home** is important. But what happens when you don't have a lot of money to buy? Here are two interesting options for millennials.

Oscar Knight lives in a new apartment in an exciting **neighborhood** in London. "This is an **apartment building** designed for young people between the ages of 20 and 35," he says. "We live, work, and play all in one space. It's not boring at all! There are different spaces for us to use, such as a library, a community **garden**, a gym, an office, a popular restaurant, and a grocery store."

"London is expensive," says Layla, one of Oscar's neighbors. "But it's a fun **city**. I pay £330 per week here, but that includes Wi-Fi, electricity, water, and a gym. I never feel bored here. It's a great place to live, and the people are very friendly."

Eco-pod similar to Jay's eco-pod.

Jay Nilsson, from Sweden, lives in an unusual house. He has a one-room eco-pod. "This eco-pod is great," says Jay. "You can live wherever you want. My eco-pod is in my parents' **yard** on a quiet **street**, but I can move my eco-pod, too." Eco-pods are not cheap—Jay's eco-pod cost him almost $93,000. They are also very small—only 8 meters long. But there is a bed, a bathroom, and a tiny kitchen. It's good for one person only!

1 What city does Oscar live in? ____________
2 Does Layla think it is a good place for young people to live? ____________
3 Where does Jay live? ____________
4 How big is Jay's eco-pod? ____________

C **IN PAIRS THINKING SKILL—Apply** **Discuss your preferences and explain. Do you want to live in an apartment building like Oscar or in an eco-pod like Jay?**

VOCABULARY

A **Complete the definitions with words from the article.**

1 a place to live: h____________, a____________
2 an area around a house: g____________, y____________
3 the area around where you live: n____________
4 the people who live near you: n____________
5 a very large town: c____________
6 a road: s____________

MAKE IT YOURS

Find more words that describe your neighborhood and the house, apartment, or street where you live.

GRAMMAR adjectives

A Circle adjectives in READING B.

B Read the grammar rules. Complete the examples from READING B.

1 Use adjectives to describe nouns. Adjectives often come before a noun. Write three examples from the text.
a new apartment, ______, ______, ______
2 Adjectives can also come after the verbs *be*, *look*, or *feel*. Write one example from the text.
London is expensive. ______
3 Some adjectives end in *–ing* and describe things or places. Write one example from the text.
an exciting neighborhood, ______
4 Some adjectives end in *–ed* and describe feelings. Write one example from the text.
excited, ______

For more practice, go to page 148.

C Unscramble and write the sentences.

1 expensive / this / café / an / is / .
______
2 this / the / great / restaurant / at / popular / is / food / .
______
3 neighbors / very / noisy / my / are / .
______
4 class / boring / really / is / this / a / .
______

D IN PAIRS Discuss your neighborhoods using adjectives.

A: What's your neighborhood like? *B: It's quiet. How about yours?*

PRONUNCIATION syllable stress in multi-syllable adjectives

A 5.02 Say the words. Underline the stressed syllable. Then listen and check.

1 lively quiet busy
2 expensive exciting important

B 5.03 Listen and notice how the stressed syllable is louder and longer than the unstressed syllables. Practice stressing the syllables.

1 expensive houses 2 an exciting city 3 busy neighborhood

SPEAKING

A Write two sentences that are true and one sentence that is not true about your home and neighborhood.

B IN GROUPS Read your sentences aloud. Ask your group members to guess which sentence is not true. Use the Confident Communicator box to help you.

CONFIDENT COMMUNICATOR
KEEP TALKING

When you're not sure about something, you can make guesses:
It's just a guess, but …
It's difficult to say, but …
I bet it's …

LESSON 2

What's in Your Neighborhood?

VOCABULARY places in a neighborhood

A Write the places under the pictures with words from the box. Compare your answers with a partner.

apartment building	bus stop	coffee shop	grocery store
gym	high school	library	train station

1 

2 

3 

4 

5 

6 

7 

8 

B Use words from A to complete the table.

Places to …

live/study	exercise	shop	travel to/from	hang out

MAKE IT REAL

Sometimes you hear different words for the same places in a neighborhood.

gym = fitness center, health club

grocery store = supermarket

coffee shop = café

apartment (American English) = flat (British English)

LISTENING

A Look at the pictures. Would you like to live in these neighborhoods?

B 5.04 **LISTENING SKILL—Listen for specific information** **Listen to the radio show. Check (✓) the places Elsa and Ahmed mention.**

	coffee shop	park	gym	bus stop	train station	grocery store	library	apartment building	high school
Elsa									
Ahmed									

C 5.04 **Listen again. Who likes their neighborhood? Discuss.**

D **IN PAIRS THINKING SKILL—Evaluate** **Compare and discuss where you want to live.**

1 What are the differences between living outside of a town or city and living close to the city?
2 Where do you like to live?

GRAMMAR *there is / there are*

A **Read the sentences. Complete the rules.**

There is a grocery store and a park.
There's no gym and no library.
Are there things to do or places to hang out in your neighborhood?
There's a coffee shop where I hang out with my friends.

1 We use *There is* and *There are* to talk about **things that exist** / **things that don't exist**.
2 We use *There is no* and *There are no* to talk about **things that exist** / **things that don't exist**.
3 *Are there ...?* is the question form for **one thing** / **more than one thing**.
4 *There's* is the contraction of ***there is*** / ***there are***.

For more practice, go to page 148.

B **Find one mistake and write the correct sentences.**

1 There aren't a train station near my house. ______
2 Are there a gym in your neighborhood? ______
3 In my town, there a grocery store, but no library. ______
4 There's not coffee shop in my neighborhood. ______
5 There are a good restaurant near the bus stop. ______

C **Make notes about your neighborhood and what amenities you think it needs. Share with a partner.**

D **As a class, discuss your neighborhoods.**

SPEAKING

A **Draw a map of a neighborhood with at least six places on it in your notebook.**

B **IN PAIRS** **Discuss your maps. Use the Confident Communicator box to help you.**

Do not look at your partner's map. When your partner asks about a place on your map, put a check (✓). When your partner asks about all the places on your map, say *Bingo!* The first pair to find all the places on both maps wins.

A: Is there a library?
B: No, there's no library. / Yes, there's a library.

CONFIDENT COMMUNICATOR
KEEP TALKING

Visitors often need information about a place from a person who knows the area. To say you know or don't know an area, say:
I'm from (near) here.
I'm (not) a local.
I'm (not) from around here.
I (don't) live close by.

Are You Lost?

VOCABULARY directions

A Match the directions to the pictures. Write the letters.

1 Take the first left. ____
2 Turn around. ____
3 Take the second left. ____
4 Go straight ahead. ____

B Look at the map. Write the answer.

1 It's next to the apartment building. __________
2 It's between the apartment building and the gym. __________
3 It's across from the grocery store. __________
4 It's on the corner of River Street and Third Avenue. __________

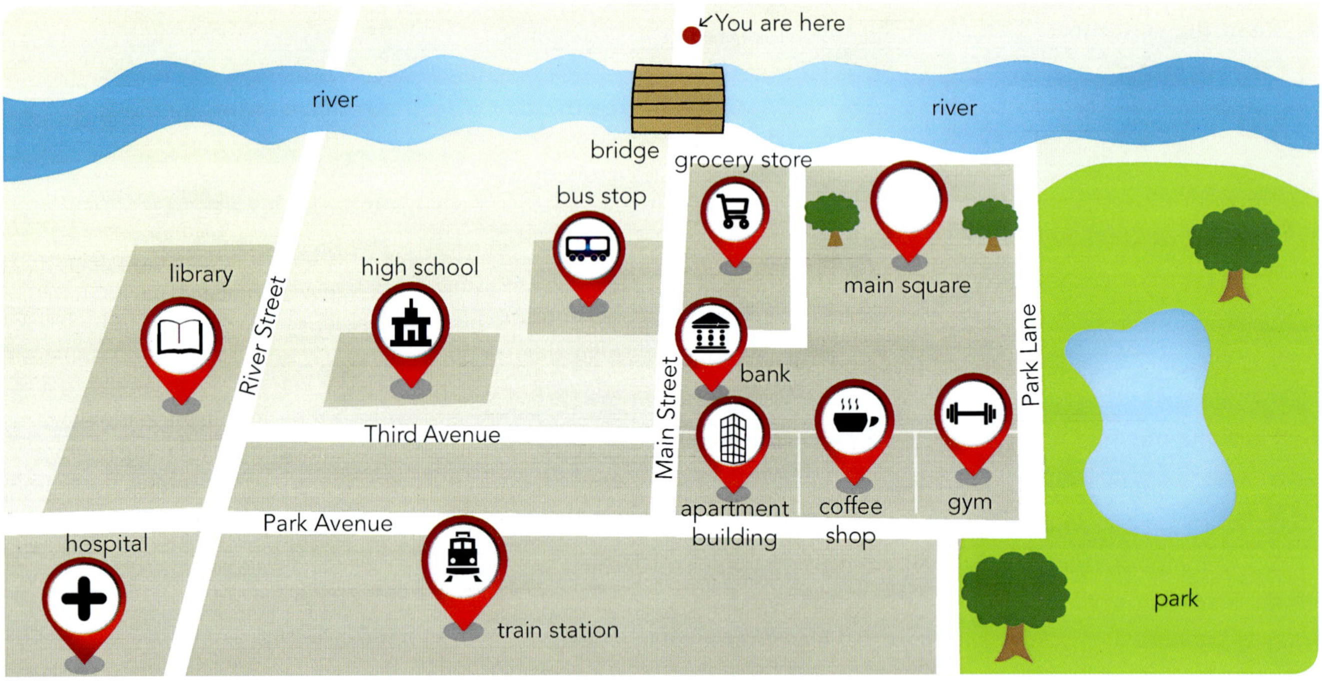

C Look at the map in B again. Then complete the directions.

1 A: Excuse me. How do I get to the high school? B: Go over the bridge. Then take the first __________.
2 A: Can you tell me how to get to the train station? B: Yes. Go __________ and then take the second right.
3 A: Is there a bus stop near here? B: It's over there, across from the __________.
4 A: How do I get to the library? B: Take the next __________. Then take another right.
5 A: Hi. Do you know where the coffee shop is? B: Yes. It's __________ the apartment building and the gym.

D IN PAIRS Discuss directions. Ask for and give directions to and from the places.

1 from the library to the bus stop
2 from the train station to the coffee shop
3 from the apartment building to the high school
4 from the park to the library

LISTENING

A IN PAIRS Check (✓) what you do if you get lost.

☐ call a friend or relative
☐ ask a person on the street for help
☐ keep walking or driving
☐ use a map on your phone

B 5.05 LISTENING SKILL—Listen for key words **Listen to the conversations. Write the places the speakers want to go to.**

1 Conversation 1: ____________________

2 Conversation 2: ____________________

3 Conversation 3: ____________________

4 Conversation 4: ____________________

5 Conversation 5: ____________________

C 5.05 **Listen again and write the directions in your notebook.**

D IN PAIRS THINKING SKILL—Analyze **Discuss.**

1 Where do you sometimes get lost?
2 What do you do?
3 Do you ask for help? Who do you ask?
4 How often do you get lost?

WRITING

A **Read the instant messages. Does Samantha know how to get to the coffee shop? Discuss.**

B **Match the words from the box to the abbreviations.**

Samantha:
Hi! How RU? Meet for coffee tomorrow?

Melissa:
Sure. Baker's? 4 p.m.?

Samantha:
OK. Send directions!

Melissa:
Main St. to 3 Ave. Cross the bridge. Turn left at Harry's. Take next right. Baker's bldg is on the corner. CU 2morrow!

building	tomorrow	are you
see you	avenue	street

1 Ave ____________
2 2morrow ____________
3 CU ____________
4 RU ____________
5 bldg ____________
6 St ____________

C **Rewrite the instant messages in complete sentences in your notebook. Don't use abbreviations.**

D IN PAIRS **Practice writing directions. Text or write directions to your partner using abbreviations and/or emojis. Then write your partner's directions in complete sentences.**

SPEAKING

A IN PAIRS **Practice the conversation. Use the Confident Communicator box to help you.**

A: Excuse me. Where is the bus stop?

B: It's straight ahead. Go one more block.

B IN PAIRS **Role-play asking for and giving directions. Then change roles and role-play again.**

Student A: You are lost. Ask how to get to places from your school.
Student B: Give directions to Student A.

CONFIDENT COMMUNICATOR
START TALKING

To ask for directions, say:
Excuse me. Where is/are …?
How do I get to …?
Can you tell me where the … is/are?
Is there a/an … nearby?

Language and Life

Problem-solving – A Neighborhood Guide

A 5.06 Read the magazine article. Is Katy happy in her new neighborhood? Discuss.

A New Place to Call Home

Name: Katy Morgan
From: Austin, Texas

I'm Katy. I'm from the United States, but now I live in a small neighborhood outside Cusco, Peru. Cusco is an amazing city. Machu Picchu is very close by. I have my own business here. I organize eco-tours around the area.

Life in Peru is great. I speak Spanish, so communication isn't a problem. There are other differences. In the States, things happen fast and people run from place to place. Here, life is slow, and I like it that way!

My neighborhood is small, but there are stores, restaurants (amazing food!), and a beautiful main square (the Plaza de Armas) in the city center. I live in a one-bedroom apartment on a quiet street. There's a small coffee shop across from my house, so I hang out with my neighbors before work. People here like to get together and talk.

It's hard to find a place to live when you arrive in a new city. There's a great company called Home Abroad Rentals. They find apartments for people from other countries who are new to Cusco. They match people to the right home. I'm happy Cusco is the place I call home.

B **Read the profiles of people who want to find a place to live in your city. Make notes about neighborhoods that are good for each person, and say why those places are good.**

Profile 1

Name: James Quigley

Age: 28

From: Johannesburg, South Africa

Job: translator for a large tech company

Prefers: to live outside the town/city center; to live alone

Wants to find: a small house with a yard

Hobbies: swimming, cooking, going out to eat, seeing friends, biking

follow

Profile 2

Name: Christine Summers

Age: 23

From: Sydney, Australia

Job: English teacher

Prefers: to live in the town/city center; to have roommates

Wants to find: a one-bedroom apartment; a shared house

Hobbies: dancing, running, reading, traveling

follow

C **IN PAIRS** **Compare your ideas for the profiles.**

A: I think a good neighborhood for Christine is … because there's a park.

B: I think … is a good neighborhood for James because there are houses with yards.

D **IN PAIRS** **Complete a neighborhood guide for an area you know well.**

Neighborhood guide for: ______________________

Types of housing available: ______________________

Sports facilities: ______________________

Popular restaurants: ______________________

Good places to shop: ______________________

How to get around (bus/train): ______________________

Directions from housing to one or two other interesting places: ______________________

____

____

E **IN GROUPS** **Discuss your guides. Then share with the class.**

MAKE IT DIGITAL

Go online and look for more information about the neighborhood. Include any information you think is useful.

VOCABULARY review

SCORE: / 10

A Complete the sentences with words from the box.

across	boring	expensive	on	square
apartment	difficult	gym	popular	tiny

Jasper: I live near the university. There are many students here, so it's not an expensive part of town. I live in an old **1** ________ with only one room. It's **2** ________ , but it's OK for me.

Kate: I live with my parents. It's a big house near the main **3** ________ in town, but there is nothing fun to do in the neighborhood. It's **4** ________ .

Ed: I have a new apartment **5** ________ the corner of Main and First. I like it, but I pay a lot—about $1,300 a month. It's a very **6** ________ neighborhood.

Kim: I love my neighborhood. There are fun coffee shops, great restaurants, and a new **7** ________ to work out in. The neighborhood is **8** ________ with students and families.

Neil: My new house is on Third Street. From here, cross the bridge and then turn left. It's **9** ________ from the park. It's not **10** ________ to find.

GRAMMAR review

SCORE: / 10

A Combine the two sentences into one.

1 Cusco is a city. Cusco is exciting.

____

1 It's a place. It's friendly.

____

2 There are many neighborhoods. They're lively.

____

3 There's a market. It's very interesting.

____

4 Cusco has some buildings. They're very old.

____

B Match the sentence beginning (1–5) to the sentence end (a–e). Write the letter.

1 There are ____ **a** many Cuban restaurants?
2 There is ____ **b** an airport near the city?
3 There's no ____ **c** people from all over the world.
4 Is there ____ **d** train to Everglades National Park.
5 Are there ____ **e** a zoo with lots of different animals.

16–20 correct: You can talk about places in a neighborhood and give directions. You can use adjectives and *there is/there are*.
0–15 correct: Look again at the Vocabulary and Grammar sections in the unit.

TOTAL SCORE: / 20

WHAT DO YOU KNOW NOW? Look back at page 47 and add the words you know now to the boxes.

STUDY SKILLS RESEARCH SKILLS

Take the quiz about research skills. Go to **Study Skills** on page 131 to find the answers. Then learn more about research skills.

1 About … people around the world work full-time as researchers.
a 5.3 million **b** 7.8 million **c** 10 million

2 It takes the average person … to read one page.
a one minute **b** two minutes **c** three minutes

3 Only 12% of teachers say their students use books for research.
a true **b** false

4 About 95% of internet users believe that most or all of the information they find online is true.
a true **b** false

UNIT 6 Going Viral

WHAT DO YOU ALREADY KNOW?

1 **Think of words about social media and the internet. Write the words or draw the icons of apps you use.**

2 **IN PAIRS** **Share and compare your information. Add more words to your lists.**

Social media

Internet

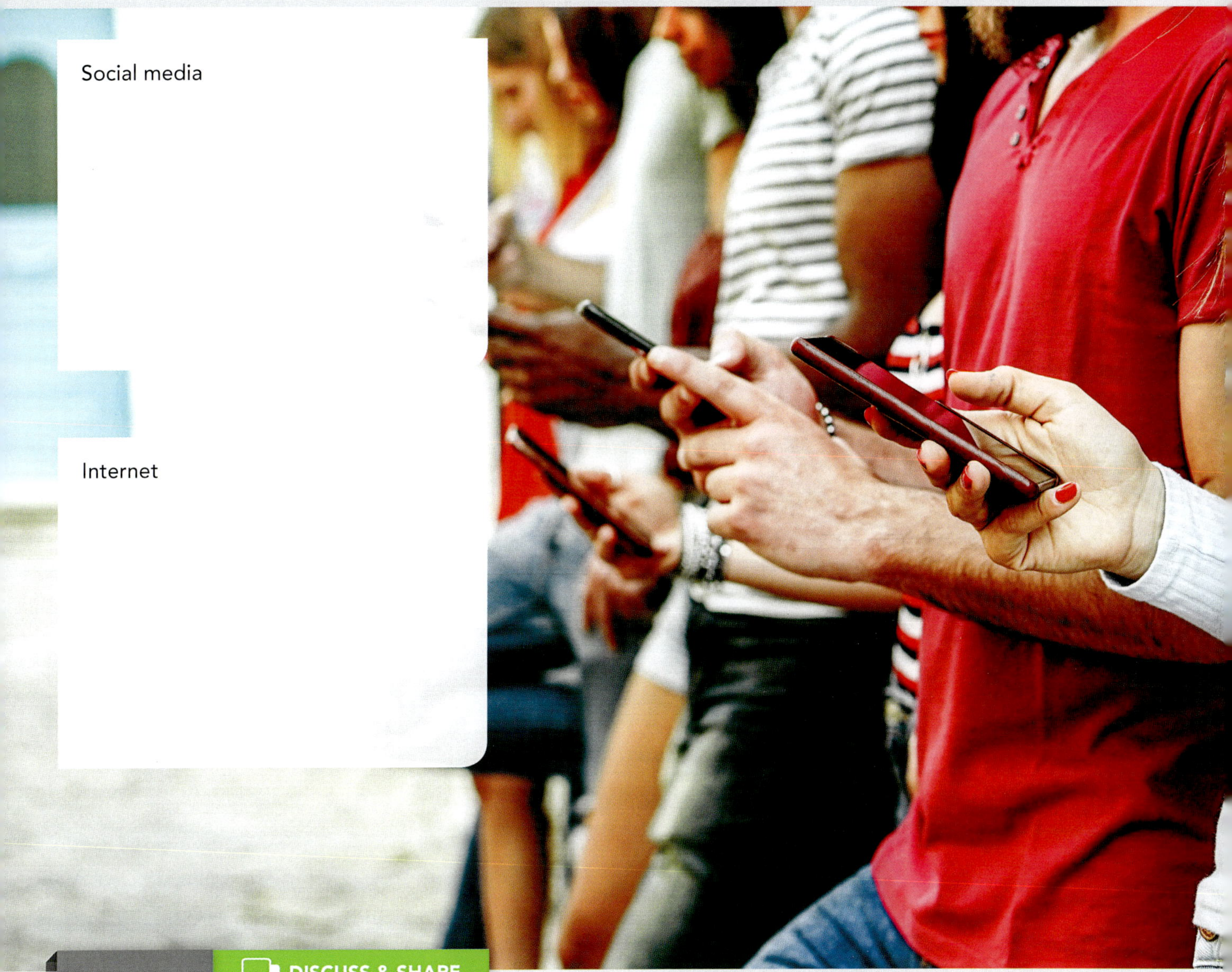

DISCUSS & SHARE

VIDEO

3 **IN GROUPS** **Watch the video and answer the question.**

SYM How much time do you spend online?

In this unit, you will ...

- talk about media use, computer equipment, and online business.
- use thinking skills: analyze and evaluate.
- read about social media use and employment.
- use strategies to keep talking by showing interest and asking follow-up questions.
- use critical thinking skills to analyze the pros and cons of a digital detox.
- follow a social media marketing manager to learn about this job and the skills needed for this industry.

You and Social Media

READING

A **IN PAIRS** **Discuss the social media apps you use and how often you use them.**

A: I use … every day. *B: I never use …*

B **6.01 READING SKILL—Predict information** **Read the article and guess the missing information. Then check your answers below.**

Social Media Use and Employment

Do some things about social media make you **angry**?
If your answer is "yes," read on …

Young adults are spending a lot of time on social media these days. According to Statista, about **1** ______________ billion people use social media. Are you **surprised**? That's about one-third of the world's population! In the US, around **2** ______________% of people aged 16 to 24 have social media accounts. On average, they spend **3** ______________ minutes per day—almost two hours—on social media. **4** ______________ has more social media users than any other country—596 million. That number is growing all the time.

Many people are **afraid** that employers are getting information about them from social media. This information can make them feel **embarrassed**.

A study by Statista from 2017 shows that **5** ______________% of employers look at social media profiles before they hire someone. So, be very careful and check your settings. Keep your social media profiles for family and friends only.

Read more

Answer Key for Reading B:
1 2.5; **2** 98; **3** 109; **4** China; **5** 61

VOCABULARY

A **Read the sentences (1–4) and match the words in bold to the emojis (a–d). Write the letter.**

1. 2.5 billion people use social media! Really? I'm **surprised**! _____
2. I'm **embarrassed** when I tell people I don't use social media. _____
3. I'm **mad** when there are ads on social media sites all the time. _____
4. Don't be **afraid** to take a break from social media. _____

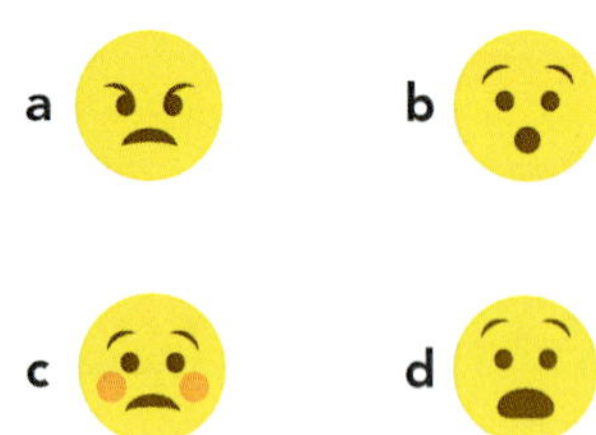

B **THINKING SKILL—Analyze** **Which of these opinions do you agree with? Why?**

1. Social media friends are not real friends.
2. Social media is a great way to share information.

MAKE IT YOURS

Which emojis do you use most often? Send an emoji to a classmate to say how you are feeling. Ask that person to say in English how you are feeling.

GRAMMAR present progressive

A Read the examples. Then choose the correct option to complete the rules.

Young adults are spending a lot of time on social media these days.
Employers are now using social media sites.
They're getting information about future employees.

1. Use the present progressive for things that are happening **every day** / **now**.
2. Form the present progressive with the verb *be* + **–*ing*** / **infinitive**.
3. When a verb ends in –*e*, remove –*e* and add –*ing*: *use* becomes *using*, *take* becomes ***takeing*** / ***taking***.
4. When a verb ends in a vowel + consonant, double the last consonant and add –*ing*: *get* becomes *getting*, *stop* becomes ***stopping*** / ***stoping***.
5. When a verb ends in –*ie*, change the –*ie* to –*y* and add –*ing*: *lie* becomes *lying*, *tie* becomes ***tying*** / ***tieing***.

For more practice, go to page 149.

B Complete the conversation with the present progressive.

Jenny: Hi, Gemma. **1** What ____________ you ____________ (do)?
Gemma: **2** Oh, I ____________ (look) at things online.
Jenny: **3** Why____________ you ____________? (not study)
Gemma: **4** I ____________ (take) a break. So what's up?
Jenny: **5** I ____________ (call) because I need help.
Gemma: Are you worried about the exam tomorrow?
Jenny: **6** No, I ____________ (buy) some new shoes online. Can you look at them?
Gemma: Sure!

C IN PAIRS Role-play a phone conversation. Talk about what you are doing now and how you are feeling.

SPEAKING

A Complete the table with the things you are usually doing at these times and days.

	Tuesday	Friday	Saturday
7 a.m.			
12 p.m.			
6 p.m.			
11 p.m.			

B IN PAIRS Ask and answer questions about what you are doing at these times. Use the Confident Communicator box to help you.

A: It's 7 a.m. on Sunday. What are you doing?
B: I'm sleeping.
A: And how are you feeling?
B: I'm relaxed!

CONFIDENT COMMUNICATOR
START TALKING

To ask about feelings, say: *Are you OK? Is everything all right? What's the matter?*
To describe how you are feeling, say: *I'm feeling … today. / I'm sad about … / I'm happy about … / I'm tired / I'm sleepy / I'm hungry.*

LESSON 2 Vlogging

VOCABULARY technology equipment

A Match the words from the box to the pictures.

microphone	headphones	keyboard	screen
smartphone	mouse	tablet	webcam

1 
____

2 
____

3 
____

4 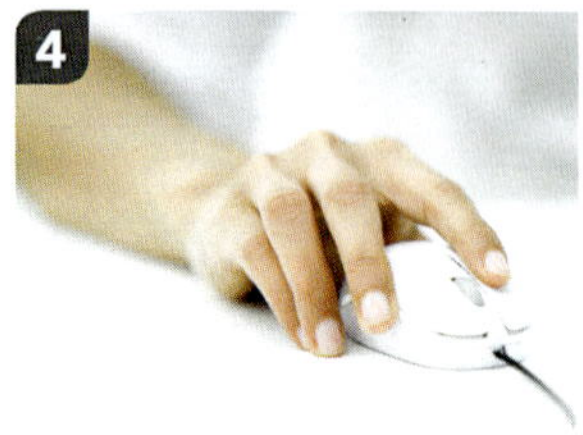
____

5 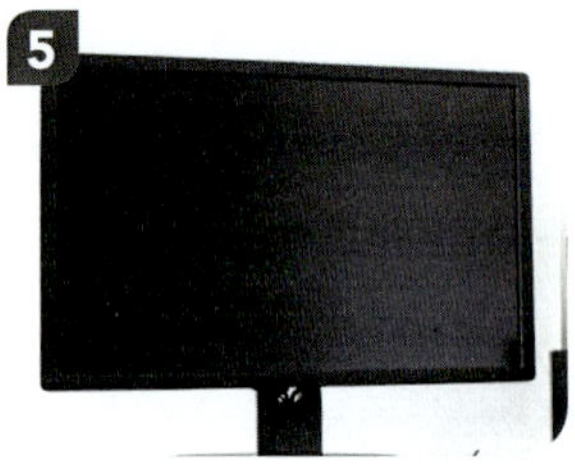
____

6 
____

7 
____

8 
____

B Complete the information about vlogging with the words in the box.

microphone smartphone tablets webcam

So, you want to be a vlogger?

Here are some of the things you need.

To film your vlog, you need a video camera. If you are sitting at home with your computer, you can use the **1** ______________. Some vloggers use the camera on their **2** ______________ to make videos. The screens are very small, but they work fine. **3** ______________ are also OK to use, but a computer makes your vlog look more professional. When you speak, you use a **4** ______________. People need to hear what you are saying, so get a good one.

Happy vlogging!

MAKE IT YOURS

Compound words are two different words put together.

desk + *top* = *desktop*

web + *camera* = *webcam*

What other compound words do you know?

LISTENING

A IN PAIRS Match vlog types from the box to the pictures.

computer gaming food product reviews travel

1 
____

2 
____

3 
____

4 
____

B 6.02 **Listen to the vloggers and match them to the vlog types in A.**

1 Speaker 1: ____________
2 Speaker 2: ____________
3 Speaker 3: ____________
4 Speaker 4: ____________

C 6.03 **LISTENING SKILL—Listen for fact and opinion Listen and choose *Fact* or *Opinion*.**

1 Fact / Opinion
2 Fact / Opinion
3 Fact / Opinion
4 Fact / Opinion
5 Fact / Opinion

D THINKING SKILL—Evaluate Discuss the statement. Do you agree? What do you think makes a good vlogger?

A good vlogger is like the boy or girl next door—someone who feels like I do about things.

GRAMMAR present progressive vs. simple present

A Read the sentences. Underline the present progressive verbs. Circle the simple present verbs.

1 Right now, I'm using my laptop to upload videos …
2 I spend about six months of the year away from home …
3 I'm studying to be a computer programmer.
4 People always ask me for advice …

B Choose the correct option to complete the rules.

1 We use the simple present to talk about things that happen **regularly** / **now or around now**.
2 We use the present progressive to talk about things that are happening **regularly** / **now or around now**.

For more practice, go to page 150.

C Choose the correct option. Is the question in simple present or present progressive?

1 Where is your laptop?
a simple present **b** present progressive
2 What are you watching on your laptop?
a simple present **b** present progressive
3 What kind of camera do you use to make vlogs?
a simple present **b** present progressive
4 What famous vloggers are you following?
a simple present **b** present progressive

D IN PAIRS Ask and answer the questions from C.

SPEAKING

A Write complete questions in your notebook with the words given.

1 What / do / do?
2 What / do / generally / vlog / about?
3 How / usually / make / your vlog?
4 How / often / vlog?

B IN PAIRS Role-play. Use the Confident Communicator box to help you.

Student A: Imagine you are a well-known music vlogger.
Student B: Imagine you are a famous skateboarding vlogger. Ask and answer questions in A to find out more about your partner.

C IN GROUPS Discuss which vlogs you watch. Do you have your own vlog?

CONFIDENT COMMUNICATOR
KEEP TALKING

It's important to show interest when someone is talking to you:
Oh, right. *I see.* *Uh-huh.* *Really?*
When things are very interesting, your voice is usually higher and louder:
No way! *Wow, that's amazing!* *You're kidding!*

LESSON 3 Buying and Selling Online

LISTENING

A Check (✓) the things you like to buy and sell in online stores.

- ☐ books
- ☐ clothes
- ☐ electronics (smartphones, headphones)
- ☐ music, movies, video games
- ☐ sports equipment (soccer balls, athletic shoes, baseball bats)
- ☐ other: ______________________________

B 6.04 LISTENING SKILL—Listen for the main idea Listen to an interview with an internet business owner. Then answer the question.

1 What does he buy and sell? __________

C 6.04 Listen again and answer the questions.

1 How old is Luca?
2 Where does he buy and sell things?
3 How much money does he make per item?
4 How often does Luca add new pictures to his website?
5 What is his day job?

D THINKING SKILL—Evaluate Consider some of the differences between shopping online and shopping in a store. What do you prefer? Why?

I like shopping in a store because I can see and touch what I'm buying.

VOCABULARY technology phrases

A 6.05 Listen and complete the phrases with words from the box.

go post send take update upload

1 __________ a text message
2 __________ pictures
3 __________ comments
4 __________ my profile
5 __________ viral
6 __________ a selfie

B Match the phrases from A (1–6) to the definitions (a–f). Write the number.

a take a picture of yourself on a smartphone ____
b write your opinion about something online ____
c communicate by typing on your smartphone ____
d become very popular on the internet ____
e copy a picture to the internet ____
f put new information about yourself on a social media site ____

PRONUNCIATION /ŋ/

A 6.06 Listen and notice the /ŋ/ sound for the letters *–ng*.

1 kin king
2 sin sing
3 thin thing

B 6.07 IN PAIRS Listen and practice saying the sentences. Is your partner using the /ŋ/ sound correctly?

1 Sing this song.
2 The teacher is talking.
3 I'm listening to music.

WRITING

A Check (✓) the details to include when you want to sell a product online.

- ☐ information about the product (name, type, color)
- ☐ what it does (takes pictures, plays music, etc.)
- ☐ where it is from
- ☐ condition (excellent, good, used, never used, etc.)
- ☐ why you're selling it
- ☐ the price

B Read and compare the two social media ads. Then discuss the questions.

1 Which ad do you like more?
2 Which ad makes you want to buy the headphones?

A

A pair of headphones for sale. They are good for listening to music. They are white. They are in good condition. They come from China. They cost $60. I am selling them for $45 because I want the money to buy new headphones.

follow

B

Hi! I'm selling my BodeA345 headphones. White. They're amazing! Fantastic sound. Very comfortable. Excellent condition. $40

follow

C Write *A* or *B*.

This ad …

1 uses positive adjectives. _____
2 doesn't use complete sentences. _____
3 doesn't use the same phrases for every sentence. _____
4 gives information that isn't important. _____

D Write a social media ad for something you want to sell online in your notebook.

SPEAKING

A Write sentences in your notebook about how you use technology and how often you do it.

I upload pictures to my social media profile about once a week.
I don't take selfies on my smartphone very often.

B IN GROUPS Discuss your online activity and how you use technology. Use the Confident Communicator box to help you.

CONFIDENT COMMUNICATOR
KEEP TALKING

To keep a conversation going, it's a good idea to ask for more information. When someone gives you a *yes/no* answer, you can ask follow-up questions. They usually begin with *How*, *Where*, *When*, *What*, and *Who*.
Do you take selfies?
How often do you take them?
What social media sites do you use?

Language and Life

Critical Thinking – A Digital Detox

A 6.08 Read the article. Then answer the questions.

Digital Detox

How to Do a Digital Detox

June 21 12:10

Are you spending too much time using your phone? Check the things that are true for you to find out:

- I check social media before I get out of bed. ☐
- I send messages while I have breakfast. ☐
- I often take my phone to the bathroom. ☐
- I never go out without my phone. ☐

Did you check three or four? Then, it may be time for a digital detox. Mandy Morgan, a social media expert, gives us this advice …

"This isn't about tech devices," she explains. "It's about understanding what is healthy. People usually feel good when they don't use their smartphones all the time."

Morgan says that a seven-day detox helps with your sleep, your studies, and how you feel. She asks people to check their screen time and count how many times a day they pick up their phone.

When you do a digital detox, you don't have your phone all the time. For seven days, you practice when and where you use your smartphone. You learn to leave your phone at home sometimes.

Marcia Estefan (DJ Blade), 23, is a club DJ from Brasilia. She is also studying to be a doctor. "I use my phone all the time," she explains. "I never think about how often I look at my screen." These days Marcia doesn't use her phone often. She rarely takes it out with her in the evening. "It makes me think about how I use technology and that's a good thing."

Before the Digital Detox

Screen Time Per Day: 3 hours 20 minutes

Picks Up Her Phone: 56 times a day

After the Digital Detox

Screen Time Per Day: 1 hour 50 minutes

Picks Up Her Phone: 23 times a day

Read more

1 Mandy Morgan says tech devices are bad for your health. Yes / No
2 You do a digital detox for one month. Yes / No
3 A digital detox can help you in different areas of your life. Yes / No
4 Marcia thinks that doing a digital detox is a good idea. Yes / No

B **IN PAIRS** **Discuss the questions.**

1 How much screen time do you have every day?

2 Do you think you use your phone too much? Be honest!

C **IN GROUPS** **Consider the pros (+) and cons (–) of doing a digital detox. Add other ideas of your own.**

Pros (+)

have time to think in class

have real conversations

your ideas: ______________________________

Cons (–)

the internet helps us study/learn

we know what our family/friends are doing

your ideas: ______________________________

D **Read the digital detox rules. As a class, decide if you want to have a digital detox for one class or one day.**

Digital detox rules

- Make your classroom a phone-free zone. No phones allowed!
- Put your phone in your pocket when you are talking or eating.
- Put your phone away on your way to/from school.
- Keep your phone on airplane mode in class, or leave it at home for a day.

E **Do the digital detox and make notes about how you feel.**

MAKE IT DIGITAL

Record a video on your smartphone about how you feel after a digital detox. Share your videos as a class. What did your classmates think?

VOCABULARY review

SCORE: / 10

A Choose the correct option.

1 Do you want to play / go / take a selfie with me?
2 I'm very afraid / mad / embarrassed. My new printer doesn't work.
3 Please post / download / take a comment after you read my blog.
4 I always use my smartphone to play / send / do a text message.
5 Please use my laptop to create / play / go an online profile.
6 It's easy to download an app with this headphones / tablet / webcam.
7 I sometimes use my desktop to go / read / upload a picture.
8 I'm surprised / afraid / embarrassed. She is giving away her new song.
9 I be / use / update my profile online once or twice a month.
10 Look into your mouse / webcam / keyboard to make a video.

GRAMMAR review

SCORE: / 10

A Complete the conversation with the correct simple present or present progressive form of the verb in parentheses.

Clare: Hey! What **1** ______________ you ______________ (do)?
Matt: Not much. I **2** ______________ (watch) a movie. You?
Clare: I **3** ______________ (study) at the library.
Matt: Again?
Clare: You know I usually **4** ______________ (come) here after class. Quick question: **5** ______________ you ______________ (use) headphones with your laptop?
Matt: Sure. I **6** ______________ (use) them right now.
Clare: What kind?
Matt: They're called AudioPlus. Electronics World **7** ______________ (sell) them.
Clare: Good to know. I need some. The people here are noisy! They **8** ______________ (talk) a lot. They **9** ______________ (not study)!
Matt: Well, get these. They always **10** ______________ (work) great!
Clare: Thanks! Gotta go—see you tomorrow.

16–20 correct: You can talk about emotions and technology. You can use the present progressive and simple present.
0–15 correct: Look again at the Vocabulary and Grammar sections in the unit.

TOTAL SCORE: / 20

WHAT DO YOU KNOW NOW? Look back at page 57 and add the words you know now to the box.

FOLLOW A PRO MARKETING

Take the quiz about marketing. Go to **Follow A Pro** on page 132 to find the answers. Then learn more about the marketing field.

1 In New York, around … people work in marketing full-time.
a 17,000 **b** 31,000 **c** 52,000

2 More customers go to a website when the company has a regular blog.
a true **b** false

3 How do 90% of businesses respond when customers complain?
a by social media **b** by email **c** by phone

4 When customers have a bad experience with a company, about 4% complain. What do the other 96% do?
a They buy the product again. **b** They tell their friends. **c** They never buy from that company again.

UNIT 1

STUDY SKILLS

A Read about memory strategies. People remember new information in different ways. Which way is best for you?

MEMORY STRATEGIES

Ricardo I use different colors to take notes in my notebook because it helps me learn. Nouns are in red, verbs are in green, and adjectives are in yellow.

Maya I love art, and I make pictures with new words and phrases. After that, I don't forget them!

Sol I learn words that go together. So, I write down family words together, words for colors together, and words for jobs together.

Meera When I learn a new word, I write it down 10 times. That helps me to remember it!

Ana I make a sentence that's true for me with the new word. So, if I learn the word *swim*, then my sentence is "I swim every Saturday," because that's true for me.

Bob I talk about my learning with my friends and tell them the new words I know. I don't like learning things alone!

B Match the example (1–6) to the memory strategy (a–f). Write the letter.

a writing new words 10 times
b sharing learning with friends
c making sentences with new words
d using different colors
e making pictures to learn things
f learning words that go together

1 *player play playful* ______

2 *hand*  ______

3 *mother, father, sister, brother, aunt, uncle* ______

4 *beautiful, beautiful, beautiful, beautiful, beautiful, beautiful, beautiful, beautiful, beautiful, beautiful* ______

5 *I study in the library. I don't study on Sundays.* ______

6  ______

C Complete the sentences with the words from the box.

laugh stories listen

1 I record my voice saying new words. Then, I ______________.
2 I put new words together to make ______________. That helps me remember.
3 I make a funny joke out of new words. If I ______________, I remember!

MAKE IT HAPPEN

Choose 10 new words you want to learn. Use three of the memory strategies to help you learn them. With a partner, talk about the three memory strategies. Use the phrases to help you.

A: I think that it's a good idea to study with friends.

B: I agree. And I want to use colors for my notes. It's easy to remember the new words that way.

D IN PAIRS Discuss the memory strategies you want to use. Use B and C to help you.

A: I want to sing the new words I learn because I love music.

B: That's a good idea. I don't like singing, so I want to make stories from the new words I learn.

E THINKING SKILL—Remember Observe what kind of memory you have.

1 Do you have a good memory for some things and not others?
2 What are some things that are difficult to memorize?
3 When do you need a good memory at your job?

Answers to the quiz on page 16
1 a 2 b 3 a 4 c

UNIT 2

FOLLOW A PRO

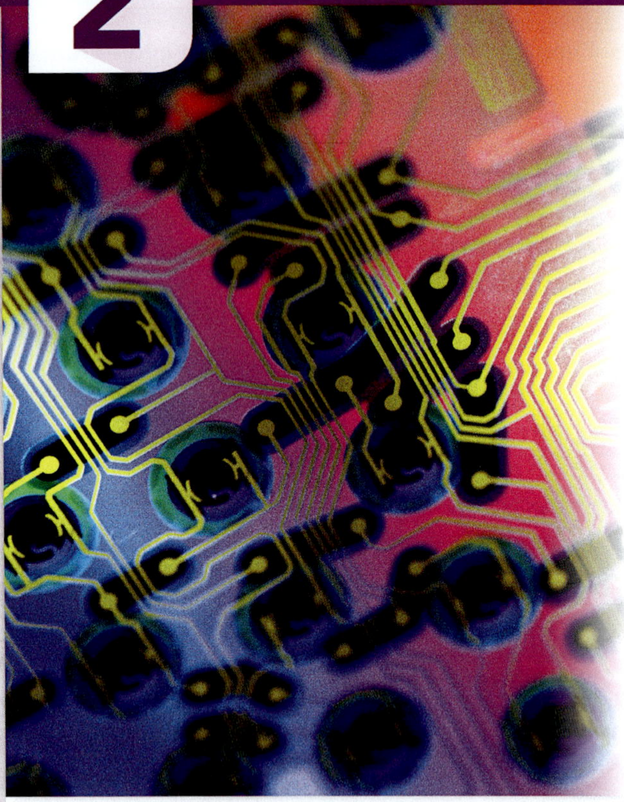

A Read about an IT consultant's job. Answer the questions below.

AN IT CONSULTANT

My name is Tim Watkins. I'm an IT consultant at my family's company, IT Computer Consultants. Our office is in the city center, not too far from my apartment. I help people with their computer problems. My sister is an accountant. She works with the company accounts. Her husband, Bob, is a computer technician. He has a degree in computer engineering. My mom is creative, and she likes to write. She's the social media marketing manager. She manages our website, writes our blog, and posts on social media. My dad is friendly and organized. He's the general manager. It's a good business and it does really well. I like working with my family.

1 Whose business is IT Computer Consultants? ______
2 What does Tim help people with? ______
3 Who is Bob? ______
4 Why is Tim's mom the social media marketing manager? ______
5 What does Tim's dad do? ______

B Discuss the questions as a class.

1 Is a family business a good idea? Why or why not?
2 Can you imagine your own family business?

VIDEO

WATCH THE VIDEO AND FOLLOW AN IT PROFESSIONAL.

C IN GROUPS Answer the questions.

1 What job is the video about? ______
2 Who does the job? ______
3 What special skills or education does this person have? ______
4 Does this person like the job? ______
5 What are some of the good and bad things about the job? ______
6 How does this person use English at work? ______

D IN GROUPS Check your answers to the quiz on page 24 and discuss the questions.

1 Do you know people who work in IT?
2 What other IT jobs do you know?
3 Do you want this kind of job? Why or why not?
4 Is there an opportunity to have this kind of job where you live?
5 What skills does an IT professional need?

Answers to the quiz on page 26
1 a 2 b 3 c 4 c

UNIT 3

STUDY SKILLS

A Read the oral presentations. Which presentation do you think is better and why?

ORAL PRESENTATIONS

1 Ella

The teacher says we have to do a talk, so … my talk is about photography. I do it every day and I like it. I don't know why. It's fun. I like it. My camera is good—it's a Lumix. And … um … I take pictures every day, and I also take pictures on weekends. My camera is black and it's not too big. And … this is my favorite picture. Um … yeah.

2 Vanessa

Hello, everyone. I want to talk to you today about my favorite hobby, swimming. I really enjoy swimming because it makes me feel good and it gives me energy. I swim every day at the swimming pool near my house. I also swim with the school swimming club: the Dolphins. There are 10 students in the club, and we swim in competitions with other schools. I love doing that! Our teacher is Mr. Skinner. He's a great swimming teacher. I like swimming because it's fun, it's good for me, and it doesn't cost a lot of money. Thank you for listening! Any questions?

B Write *Ella* or *Vanessa* next to the sentence each person said.

1 ______________ says hello.
2 ______________ talks about a favorite hobby.
3 ______________ stops and starts when she gives her presentation.
4 ______________ explains why she likes her hobby.
5 ______________ organizes her presentation.
6 ______________ isn't sure what she is talking about.
7 ______________ doesn't finish in a clear way.

C Match the tips about oral presentations (1–6) to the explanations (a–f). Write the letter.

1 Smile and look at your listeners. _____
2 Don't speak fast. Take your time. _____
3 Plan your presentation. _____
4 Organize your presentation. Use words like *First*, *Second*, and *Next*. _____
5 Tell an interesting story. Don't just use facts and data. _____
6 Answer questions at the end of your presentation. _____

a People remember stories, but they forget facts and numbers.
b You feel nervous when you don't plan.
c Listeners need time to think as you speak.
d Your listeners feel comfortable when you are friendly.
e Your listeners can learn more when they ask questions.
f Present your ideas one at a time so your listeners can follow.

D Rewrite the first presentation in A as an interesting, clear presentation.

Hello, everyone. Welcome to my talk on photography …

E THINKING SKILL—Create Why is it a good idea to prepare and practice a presentation before you speak in public? In what jobs do you need oral presentation skills?

✓ MAKE IT HAPPEN

Prepare an oral presentation on your favorite hobby. Organize your presentation with these questions.

When do you do your hobby?
Why do you like it?
Where do you do your hobby?
Who do you do your hobby with?

Answers to the quiz on page 36
1 b (You need to spend 70% of your time on writing.) 2 c 3 c 4 b

UNIT 4

FOLLOW A PRO

A **Read about a firefighter's job. Answer the questions below.**

A FIREFIGHTER

Sally Lane is a firefighter. She is at the fire station 24 hours a day for three days, and then she has three days off. On her workdays, Sally sleeps at the fire station. She gets up at 4:00 a.m., gets dressed, and eats breakfast with the other firefighters. She takes a shower in the evening, not in the morning. Sally usually works at least 15 hours on a workday. She fights fires, practices with the equipment, goes to the fire station gym, and takes online classes to learn new information about fighting fires. Sally's job is difficult, but she likes it. She says, "I love my job because the work is always exciting and interesting. I like to help people. It's not always easy. When we are busy, I don't have time to eat or sleep!"

1 Where does Sally sleep on workdays? ______
2 When does she get up on workdays? ______
3 Who does she eat breakfast with? ______
4 How many hours does Sally usually work? ______
5 What different things does she do at work? ______
6 Why does Sally like her job? ______

B **Discuss the questions as a class.**

1 Could you be a firefighter? Why or why not?
2 What are the good points and bad points about Sally's job?
3 There aren't many women firefighters. Why not?

VIDEO

WATCH THE VIDEO AND FOLLOW A PARAMEDIC.

C **IN GROUPS Answer the questions.**

1 What job is the video about? ______
2 What skills does the person need for the job? ______
3 Who does the person work with? ______
4 What's the most difficult part of the person's job? ______
5 Is the person happy in this job? ______
6 What is the person's work schedule? ______

D **IN GROUPS Check your answers to the quiz on page 44 and discuss the questions.**

1 Do you know any firefighters?
2 What other jobs in the emergency services do you know?
3 What are the good points and bad points of working in the emergency services?
4 What skills do you need to work in the emergency services?
5 What special physical abilities do you need to work in the emergency services?

Answers to the quiz on page 46
1 b 2 a 3 c 4 a

UNIT 5 STUDY SKILLS

A Read the texts. Who are the texts for?

RESEARCH SKILLS

Education at Morrison University

With an education major, you can study a subject you love and then teach others what you know! This major is a good choice for people who want to work with children or adults in school or college.

Courses include:

- Managing a class
- Health and well-being
- Art and creativity
- Teaching language

Good writing, math, and communication skills are necessary.

Students say:

"This major is fun! I loved it."

Prize for best education course in 1982.

99% of students at Morrison University get jobs after graduating.

Business at **Markston University**

Do you want to work in international business? With a business major, you can study how business, sales, and accounting work in different countries. Learn what you need to be successful.

Classes include:

- Marketing a product
- Growing a small business
- International business
- Social media today
- Accounting

You need math ability and a foreign language.

Students say: "This major prepares you for a life in business. I now have my own international hotel chain and it's doing very well."
—Sam Blackthorne, former student

95% of our graduates find jobs in business.

The university won "Best Business Major" in 2018.

B Write the letter *E* (Education) or *B* (Business) next to the sentences.

1. Students with this major find jobs in sales. _____
2. A student says the courses are fun. _____
3. You need to speak a foreign language to study this major. _____
4. This is a good major if you want to be a teacher. _____
5. You need good communication skills to study this major. _____

C Match the tips about research (1–5) to the reasons to do them (a–e). Write the letter.

1. Always check the date on the texts you read. _____
2. You don't always need to read every word. _____
3. Make sure the text you read was written by an expert. _____
4. Think critically about the information you find. _____
5. Write questions before you start researching. _____

a. You want the information to be correct.
b. You want to be sure that the information is up-to-date and not old.
c. Just look for the information you need—it's faster.
d. This helps you to focus on what to look for.
e. Don't believe everything you read. You have to use what you know to help you.

D Make a list of pros and cons about each of the majors in A. Share with your partner.

A: I think the education major looks good. Look! They won a prize, too.
B: Yes, but that was in 1982! I think the business major is better because …

E THINKING SKILL—Apply Do you often do research for your studies? Do you enjoy it? Why or why not? How do good research skills relate to jobs you know?

MAKE IT HAPPEN

Work with a partner. Look online and choose a major that interests you. Use the research tips in **C** to help you.

Answers to the quiz on page 56
1 a 2 b 3 b 4 b (It's 52.8%.)

UNIT 6

FOLLOW A PRO

A **Read about a chief listening officer's job. Answer the questions below.**

A CHIEF LISTENING OFFICER

What does a chief listening officer do? Dani Chavez, 29, the chief listening officer (CLO) for a soft drink company in the US, tells us about his job.

"I'm working on an idea for a new soft drink, and it's important that my company knows who buys our drinks—their age, nationality, hobbies, and so on. How do we do this? We "listen to" social media and find out what people are saying about our soft drinks. This helps us decide what products to make. Social media is very important in my job. When I see a negative comment about my company, I send that information to our Customer Service Center. They then try to understand why our customers are not happy.

Being a CLO is a new job, but there are already a lot of us. As for skills, it's very important that I have good listening skills."

1 Dani works for a …
- **a** social media company.
- **b** soft drink company.

2 "Listen to" in the text means to …
- **a** read what people are saying online.
- **b** hear what people are saying on the street.

3 What does Dani do when he sees a negative comment about his company?
- **a** He contacts the person who wrote it.
- **b** He sends the comment to the Customer Service Center.

4 A good CLO needs …
- **a** listening skills.
- **b** creative skills.

B **Discuss the questions as a class.**

1. Do you think Dani's job is interesting? Why or why not?
2. What other skills (apart from listening skills) are important for this job?
3. How can Dani's work help his company to sell more soft drinks?

VIDEO

WATCH THE VIDEO AND FOLLOW A SOCIAL MEDIA MANAGER.

C **IN GROUPS Answer the questions.**

1. What job is the video about? ______________________
2. Does the person like the job? ______________________
3. Where does the person work? ______________________
4. What is the person's favorite part of the job? ______________________
5. What is difficult about the job? ______________________
6. What does this person do for the clients? ______________________

D **IN GROUPS Check your answers to the quiz on page 64 and discuss the questions.**

1. Do you know any people who work in marketing?
2. What other jobs in marketing do you know?
3. Do you need English for this job?
4. What skills do you need to work in marketing?
5. What personal qualities do you need to work in marketing?

Answers to the quiz on page 66

1 a 2 a 3 a 4 c

Irregular Verbs

Infinitive	Simple past	Past participle
be	was/were	been
become	became	become
begin	began	begun
break	broke	broken
bring	brought	brought
build	built	built
buy	bought	bought
catch	caught	caught
choose	chose	chosen
come	came	come
cost	cost	cost
cut	cut	cut
do	did	done
draw	drew	drawn
drink	drank	drunk
drive	drove	driven
eat	ate	eaten
fall	fell	fallen
feed	fed	fed
feel	felt	felt
find	found	found
fly	flew	flown
get	got	gotten
give	gave	given
go	went	gone
grow	grew	grown
hang	hung	hung
have	had	had
hear	heard	heard
hit	hit	hit
hold	held	held
hurt	hurt	hurt
keep	kept	kept
know	knew	known
leave	left	left
let	let	let
lose	lost	lost
make	made	made
meet	met	met
pay	paid	paid
put	put	put
read	read	read
ride	rode	ridden
ring	rang	rung
rise	rose	risen
run	ran	run
say	said	said
see	saw	seen
sell	sold	sold
send	sent	sent
set	set	set
sing	sang	sung
sit	sat	sat
speak	spoke	spoken
stand	stood	stood
stick	stuck	stuck
take	took	taken
teach	taught	taught
tell	told	told
think	thought	thought
throw	threw	thrown
understand	understood	understood
wake	woke	woken
wear	wore	worn
win	won	won
write	wrote	written

Pronunciation Symbols

Vowels

ɪ	d**i**d
ɛ	b**e**d
æ	b**a**d
ʌ	c**u**p
ʊ	b**oo**k
ə	b**a**n**a**na
i	f**ee**d
ɑ	f**a**ther, b**o**x
ɔ	t**a**ll
u	st**u**dent, f**oo**d
ɝ	sh**ir**t, b**ir**thday
eɪ	d**a**te, t**a**ble
aɪ	cr**y**, **eye**
ɔɪ	b**oy**
oʊ	c**o**mb, p**o**st
aʊ	ab**ou**t, h**ow**

Consonants

p	**p**ark, ha**pp**y
b	**b**ack, ho**bb**y
t	**t**ea
d	**d**ie
k	**c**ame, **k**itchen, **q**uarter
g	**g**ame, **g**o
f	**f**ace, **ph**otogra**ph**er
V	**v**egetable
θ	**th**ing, ma**th**
ð	**th**en, **th**at
s	**c**ity, **s**ummer
z	plea**s**e, goe**s**
ʃ	**sh**e, **sh**op
ʒ	lei**s**ure
h	**h**ot, **wh**o
tʃ	**ch**icken, wa**tch**
dʒ	**j**acket, oran**g**e
m	**m**en
n	su**n**, **kn**ow
ŋ	su**ng**, si**ng**er
w	**w**eek, **wh**ite
r	**r**ain, w**r**ite**r**
l	**l**ight, **l**ong
j	**y**es, **u**se, m**u**sic

Grammar Review

A Match the sentence beginning (1–8) to the sentence end (a–h). Write the letter.

1 What's your name? ____
2 Is he your father? ____
3 Where are you from? ____
4 How old is she? ____
5 Are you and Jill from Canada? ____
6 Is her name Maria? ____
7 Who's that? ____
8 Are they Colombian? ____

a I'm from Mexico.
b No, we're not.
c That's Etsuko.
d Yes, he is.
e No, they're not.
f My name's Greg.
g Yes, it is.
h She's 18.

B Look at the picture. Complete the sentences with the words from the box.

a an any are is isn't aren't some

1 There ____________ a small bed.
2 There ____________ any pens on the desk.
3 There ____________ a laptop on the bed.
4 There ____________ some keys on the desk.
5 There's ____________ bag in front of the desk.
6 There aren't ____________ chairs.
7 There's ____________ umbrella next to the desk.
8 There are ____________ books on the bed.

C Complete the sentences with the correct form of the verb in parentheses.

1 She ____________ (work) in a large office in Chicago.
2 They ____________ (not work) on weekends.
3 I ____________ (take) the number 6 bus to school.
4 We ____________ (not live) near the train station.
5 Our school ____________ (have) a great cafeteria.
6 He ____________ (not go) to work by subway.

D Write the questions. Add *do* or *does* in the correct place.

1 you / wear a uniform / ? ______________________
2 where / they / go / after work / ? ______________________
3 your teacher / drive / to school / ? ______________________
4 that bookstore / sell / notebooks / ? ______________________
5 how / I / get to / the bus station / ? ______________________
6 who / she / study with / on weekends / ? ______________________

E Rewrite the sentences with the words in parentheses.

1 They are late for class. (often) ______________________
2 I do laundry at night. (sometimes) ______________________
3 My sister cleans the house. (hardly ever) ______________________
4 Mr. Sanchez works on Saturday. (usually) ______________________
5 We are at the office by 9:00. (always) ______________________
6 They go shopping on weekends. (never) ______________________

F Choose the correct option.

1 Eric is a good singer, but he **can't to dance** / **cannot dancing** / **can't dance** at all.
2 I **am can speak** / **can speak** / **can speaks** two languages—Spanish and English.
3 Where **do I can get** / **can I get** / **can I to get** some coffee?
4 **Can you play** / **Do you can** / **Can you playing** the piano?
5 She **can't drive** / **can't drive** / **can't drives** a car.
6 What sports **can you play** / **is it can play** / **can't you played** well?

G Complete the sentences about what is happening right now. Use the words in parentheses.

1 Kevin ______________ (read) a book.
2 Alex and Jan ______________ (not feel) well.
3 Mark and I ______________ (play) a video game.
4 It ______________ (rain).
5 Those students ______________ (not listen).
6 The teacher ______________ (check) our work.
7 It ______________ (not snow).
8 You ______________ (work) very hard.

H Choose the correct option.

Ana: Let's make **1 a** / **some** list before we go shopping.

Will: Good idea. So, what do we need?

Ana: Let's see … well, we don't have any **2 vegetables** / **vegetable**, so let's get **3 some** / **any** tomatoes and carrots.

Will: OK. And I want to make **4 an** / **some** omelet for breakfast. Do we have **5 an** / **any** eggs?

Ana: Um … yes, we do.

Will: How **6 many** / **much**?

Ana: Just two, so let's get some. And how about I make cheeseburgers for dinner?

Will: Sounds great! How **7 many** / **much** beef do you want?

Ana: Half a kilo. And don't forget the cheese. We don't have **8 any** / **some**.

Grammar Reference

UNIT 1 — *be* statements and *yes/no* questions

Function

We use *be* to talk about a name, age, job, or where someone or something is or is from. We use *yes/no* questions to ask if something is true or a fact.

Form

Affirmative		Negative	
I am (I'm)	in English 4.	I am not (I'm not)	in English 5.
You are (You're)	an English teacher.	You are not (You aren't)	a Spanish teacher.
He is (He's) She is (She's) It is (It's)	from Colombia.	He is not (He isn't) She is not (She isn't) It is not (It isn't)	from Panama.
We are (We're) They are (They're)	students.	We are not (We aren't) They are not (They aren't)	teachers.

Yes/no questions		Affirmative short answer	Negative short answer
Am I	in English 5?	Yes, you are.	No, you are not. (No, you aren't.)
Are you	a Spanish teacher?	Yes, I am.	No, I am not. (No, I'm not.)
Is he Is she Is it	from Panama?	Yes, he is. Yes, she is. Yes, it is.	No, he is not. (No, he isn't.) No, she is not. (No, she isn't.) No, it is not. (No, it isn't.)
Are we Are they	in Miami?	Yes, we are. Yes, they are.	No, we are not. (No, we aren't.) No, they are not. (No, they aren't.)

A Match the sentence beginning (1–5) to the sentence end (a–e). Write the letter.

1 She _____
2 You _____
3 They're _____
4 I _____
5 It _____

a isn't Mexican food.
b 's a Spanish teacher.
c 'm not from Canada.
d aren't in Class 5.
e from Bahia.

B Complete the sentences.

1 Are we in Class 6? Yes, we ____________.
2 Is it from Germany? No, it ____________.
3 ____________ you from Chile? Yes, I am.
4 Are they American? No, they ____________.
5 Is she a yoga teacher? Yes, she ____________.
6 ____________ your first name James? No, it isn't.

UNIT 1 — information questions with *be*

Function

We use information questions when the answer is a thing (*what?*), person (*who?*), place (*where?*), way (*how?*), or time/date (*when?*).

Form

The word order in information questions with *be* is question word + *be* + word/phrase.

Question	Answer
What is your favorite food?	My favorite food is pizza.
Who is your favorite singer?	My favorite singer is Rihanna.
Where are you from?	I'm from Guatemala.
How are you?	I'm fine.
When is your birthday?	My birthday is May 2.

A Complete the sentences with the correct *wh–* word.

1. ____________ old are you? I'm 17 years old.
2. ____________ is Manuel? He's at home.
3. ____________ is the teacher's last name? It's Sanchez.
4. ____________ is English class? It's at 10:00.
5. ____________ is your favorite actor? It's Leonardo DiCaprio.

B Choose the correct option.

1. What / Where is the teacher?
2. How / What is your email address?
3. What your hobbies are / are your hobbies?
4. Who / When is your favorite musician?
5. When / Where is her birthday?
6. How old they are / are they?

UNIT 2 — articles *a*, *an*, and no article

Function

We use the articles *a* and *an* before a noun or adjective + noun. We do not use *a* or *an* before plural nouns.

Form

Singular nouns	Plural nouns
***a* + consonant sounds (b, c, d, f, g, etc.)**	**no article**
He's a doctor. I have a small family. She studies at a university.	We're students. I have two sisters. Pilots make a lot of money.
***an* + vowel sounds (a, e, i, o, u, etc.)**	
I'm an accountant. She has an interesting job.	

A Choose *a* or *an*.

1. Paulo has a / an great job.
2. Are you a / an interior designer?
3. Sun-hee is a / an new student.
4. My father is a / an engineer.
5. I have a / an older sister.
6. A / An teacher's job is very important.

B Write *a*, *an*, or *X* (no article).

I think I have **1** ______________ interesting job. I work at **2** ______________ water park. I help **3** ______________ people at my ride. It's **4** ______________ very popular ride. Some people ride it many **5** ______________ times. I know **6** ______________ children like the ride.

UNIT 2 — possessive adjectives and *'s/s'*

Function

We use possessive adjectives and *'s/s'* to show possession or how two people are connected. Possessive adjectives and *'s/s'* agree in number with the possessor, not the thing it possesses or is connected to.

Do not confuse possessive *'s* (*Jack's sister is here.* = *His sister is here.*) with the contraction of *is* (*Jack's here.* = *Jack is here.*). Similarly, do not confuse *Whose* to ask about possession (*Whose book is this?*) with the contraction *Who's* (*Who's that?* = *Who is that?*).

Form

Possessive adjectives	
My Your His Her Its Our Their	home is small.

Add *'s* for singular and irregular nouns.
Jennifer's husband is from England. The children's teacher is Mrs. Lynn.
Add *s'* for plural nouns.
My sisters' names are Lucia and Isobel. Our parents' hometown is Los Angeles.

A Complete the sentences with the correct possessive adjective.

1. My neighbor John is from Canada. I think ______________ wife is from France.
2. I see you are from Japan. What's ______________ hometown?
3. That's Mr. and Mrs. Carlson. ______________ first names are James and Alice.
4. That's my sister. ______________ name is Jennifer. She's 16 years old.
5. My sister and I are in the same Spanish class. ______________ teacher is Mr. Cortez.
6. Hello. ______________ name is Chloe. It's nice to meet you.

B Rewrite the sentences. Add *'s* or *s'* to the correct words.

1. Tim and Marta are Susan parents. ______________________________
2. Max new friend is from India. ______________________________
3. Our grandparent home is in Florida. ______________________________
4. Their parent names are Anna and Peter. ______________________________
5. My brother wife is an interior designer. ______________________________
6. The children teacher is married. ______________________________

UNIT 3 — simple present statements and *yes/no* questions

Function

We use the simple present tense to talk about likes and dislikes, preferences, habits, and routines.

Form

Affirmative statements		**Negative statements**	
I You We They	love soccer.	I You We They	don't like baseball.
He She It	likes to watch soccer. starts at 3:30.	He She It	doesn't like to play soccer. doesn't start at 3:00.

***Yes/no* questions**			**Short answers**
Do	I you we they	need a ticket?	Yes, I do. / No, I don't. Yes, you do. / No, you don't. Yes, we do. / No, we don't. Yes, they do. / No, they don't.
Does	he she it	have a ticket? start at 3:30?	Yes, he does. / No, he doesn't. Yes, she does. / No, she doesn't. Yes, it does. / No, it doesn't.

A Choose the correct option.

Joe: Hey, Chris. **1** Do you want / Do you wants to watch the soccer game? My brother **2** has / does have a big new TV.

Chris: Umm, no, I **3** doesn't / don't. I **4** don't like / don't likes soccer. Sorry. I **5** prefer / prefers baseball. Is there a game on?

Joe: I think so, but it **6** doesn't start / don't start until 8:00.

Chris: **7** Does your brother / Do your brother like baseball?

Joe: Yes, he **8** does / doesn't. He **9** love / loves all sports.

B Complete the sentences with the correct form of the verb in parentheses.

1 My father and I ______________ (love) to watch sports together.
2 My aunt ______________ (prefer) to listen to modern music.
3 ______________ you ______________ (know) of any cool new sports apps?
4 Richie and Amelia ______________ (not like) to go to concerts.
5 ______________ your friend Mandy ______________ (want) to join our music club?
6 He's a good singer, but he ______________ (not like) to sing alone.

UNIT 3 — the imperative

Function

We use the imperative to give orders or instructions. Add *please* to sound more polite.

Form

Affirmative	Negative
Listen to this song. Please buy a ticket for me. Be happy.	Don't sit there. Please don't wait for me. Don't be sad. It's OK.

A Complete the sentences with the correct affirmative or negative form of the verbs in the box.

be buy forget go read turn up

1 ____________ to the festival before 9:00 to get good seats.
2 ____________ to call me later. I need to talk to you.
3 ____________ this book sometime. It's a very interesting story.
4 Please ____________ the music. I really want to hear this song.
5 ____________ tickets at the stadium. Get them online to save money.
6 I'm sorry about missing your party. Please ____________ angry.

UNIT 4 — simple present information questions

Function

We use a *wh–* question word to ask an information question.

Form

Information questions				Answers
Where What When	do	I you they	sit? do on weekends? get up on weekends?	You sit over there. I meet my friends. They get up at 9:00.
Why How Who	does	he she it	like his job? get to school? belong to?	He likes it because it's fun. She takes a bus. It belongs to me.

A Unscramble and write questions.

1 work / do / get to / how / they / ? ____________
2 her parents / she / when / does / talk to / ? ____________
3 eat lunch / he / where / does / every day / ? ____________
4 study with / who / do / they / ? ____________
5 does / what / he / do / in his free time / ? ____________
6 your / do / like / why / you / job / ? ____________

B Look at the answers. Write the questions.

1 Where ______________________? He works in a bank.
2 Who ______________________? We live with our parents.
3 When ______________________? Class starts at 10:00.
4 Why ______________________? She works there because it's fun.
5 How ______________________? I feel fine.
6 What ______________________? They drink coffee every morning.

UNIT 4 — frequency adverbs

Function

We use frequency adverbs to say how often we do something. Note that the adverb goes after the verb *be*, but before other verbs. The adverb *sometimes* can also go at the beginning of a sentence. (*I sometimes drive to work.* = *Sometimes I drive to work.*)

Form

Frequency adverb	Frequency	Example
always	100%	She always takes the subway to school.
usually		I usually get up at 9:00 on weekends.
often		We often eat in the school cafeteria.
sometimes		Do you sometimes listen to podcasts?
hardly ever		They are rarely in the library.
never	0%	Our teacher is never late for class.

A Choose the correct option.

My friend Adam is a real health nut. He **1 is often / often is** in the gym. He teaches a fitness class several times a week. He **2 is always / always is** early for this class. After his class, he **3 runs usually / usually runs** and lifts weights. He watches what he eats. He **4 eats rarely / rarely eats** in fast-food restaurants. He **5 has never / never has** desserts like ice cream or cake. But he **6 has sometimes / sometimes has** chocolate.

B Compete the sentences with the correct frequency adverb from the box.

always never rarely usually

1 Josh ____________ drives to work. He doesn't have a driver's license, so he always takes the bus.
2 Caroline ____________ drinks tea—maybe just once or twice a year.
3 We ____________ eat lunch in the school cafeteria. We eat there from Monday to Saturday.
4 I'm ____________ on time for class. I'm never late, so I have a perfect attendance record.

UNIT 5 — adjectives

Function

We use adjectives to add information to nouns. They can come after *be* (*The people are nice.*). They come before the noun they describe (*nice people*).

Form

After the noun	Before the noun
This café is popular.	This is a popular café.
My hometown is boring.	My hometown is a boring place.
Those houses are expensive.	Those are expensive houses.
They are very interesting.	They are very interesting people.

A Rewrite each sentence to include adjective + noun.

1. That city is dangerous. ______________________________
2. Those people are friendly. ______________________________
3. This apartment is cheap. ______________________________
4. These directions are clear. ______________________________

B Read and choose.

There are many interesting neighborhoods in São Paulo, Brazil. Take Vila Madalena, for example. The **1** lively cafés / cafés are lively, and there are excellent shops and art galleries. Make a **2** quick stop / stop quick to look at the many **3** colorful paintings / paintings colorful while you walk down the busy streets. **4** Smart shoppers / Shoppers are smart also visit the traditional markets. Here prices are low and **5** friendly people / people are friendly. Pick up some **6** fresh food / food fresh and chat with the locals.

UNIT 5 — *there is / there are*

Function

We use *there is* / *there are* to talk about things that exist.

Form

Singular	Plural
Is there a college in this city?	Are there any nice cafés near our school?
Yes, there is. / No, there isn't.	Yes, there are. / No, there aren't.
There's a library.	There are two Mexican restaurants.
There's no train station near here.	There are no good museums in this city.
There isn't a train station near here.	There aren't any good museums in this city.

A Complete the conversation with the words from the box.

Are there | Is there | There | There are | There aren't | There's

Nina: I really like Lisbon. It's a beautiful city. And the food is excellent.
Rosa: I agree. **1** ______________ some great restaurants and cafés here.
Nina: **2** ______________ any Brazilian restaurants? I love Brazilian food.
Rosa: Oh, yes. **3** ______________ any in this neighborhood. But I know one across the city.
Nina: **4** ______________ a bus we can take there? I'm so hungry!
Rosa: **5** ______________ is no bus stop near here, sorry. **6** ______________ one four or five blocks away.
Nina: Well, let's go!

UNIT 6 — present progressive

Function

We use the present progressive to talk about things that are happening now.

Form

Affirmative statements	Negative statements
I'm texting my brother.	I'm not texting my sister.
You're buying speakers.	You're not / You aren't buying headphones.
He's using his tablet.	He's not / He isn't using his computer.
She's filming with her webcam.	She's not / She isn't filming with her phone.
It's starting now.	It's not / It isn't ending now.
We're feeling surprised.	We're not / We aren't feeling embarrassed.
They're listening to a podcast.	They're not / They aren't listening to music.

Information questions		*Yes/no* questions	
What are you doing?	I'm watching a video.	Are you using your phone?	Yes, I am. / No I'm not.
Who is she texting?	She's texting her cousin.	Is he calling his parents?	Yes, he is. / No, he's not.
Why are they downloading that song?	They're downloading it because they love it.	Are they looking for the file?	Yes, they are. / No, they're not.

A Complete the sentences with the present progressive form of the verb in parentheses.

1 I ____________ (chat) with my grandparents.
2 Max ____________ (not use) his laptop right now.
3 Jill ____________ (text) her friend about the party.
4 Paul ____________ (listen) to his favorite band.
5 Wendy and Steve ____________ (not watch) the movie.
6 David and Sarah ____________ (play) video games.
7 I ____________ (not download) any songs right now.
8 Jonathan and I ____________ (wait) for your call.

B Write the question using the present progressive.

1 where / you / go / ? ____________
2 how / she / feel / ? ____________
3 why / they / smile / ? ____________
4 who / I / speaking to / ? ____________
5 what / he / do / ? ____________
6 why / we / stop / here / ? ____________

UNIT 6 — present progressive vs. simple present

Function

We use the present progressive to talk about things that are happening now or around now. We use the simple present to talk about things that happen regularly.

Form

Things that are happening now or around now	Things that happen regularly
I'm playing a video game right now.	I play video games on the weekend.
She's taking three computer classes these days.	She takes three classes every semester.
What music are you listening to right now?	What music do you like to listen to?

A Complete the sentences with the present progressive or simple present form of the verb in parentheses.

Help! **1** ____________ you ____________ (use) your flash drive? I **2** ____________ (need) one. **3** ____________ City Mall ____________ (sell) them? How much **4** ____________ they ____________ (cost)?

What **5** ____________ you ____________ (do)? My friends **6** ____________ (watch) a movie, but I **7** ____________ (not like) it. It's a romantic comedy. I **8** ____________ (prefer) action movies.

9 ____________ you ____________ (watch) the soccer game on TV? My favorite player **10** ____________ (play) in every match, but he **11** ____________ (not play) now. He **12** ____________ (sit) on the bench.

Unit 1

Track 01

International English Teachers
Your Profile

About You: I'm an English teacher in Germany. I'm from Berlin. I speak German, English, and Spanish. My hobbies are swimming, dancing, and yoga. My favorite music is rock and my favorite food is tacos (love Mexican food). My boyfriend is Juan. He isn't an English teacher. He's a yoga teacher.

Username: Berliner100
Password: DerSeestern!
Re-enter password: DerSeestern!
First name: Angela
Last name: Steiner
Nickname: Angie
Date of birth: 04/15/97
Country: Germany

Track 02

Conversation 1
Sandy: Hi, Jake!
Jake: Oh, hi, Sandy. What's up?
Sandy: Not much. Where's your wife, Michelle?
Jake: She's at work.
Sandy: Well, it's nice to see you.
Jake: Good to see you, too. Take care!
Sandy: You, too. Bye!

Conversation 2
Janice: Hello. I'm Janice Walters. I'm the office manager.
Lynn: It's nice to meet you, Ms. Walters. I'm Lynn Jefferson. I'm the new designer.
Janice: It's nice to meet you, too. Welcome to Design Associates. Please call me Janice.
Lynn: OK. Thanks, Janice.

Conversation 3
Sarah: Good morning, Mr. Wilson. Welcome to DT Bank. How are you?
Mr. Wilson: I'm fine, thank you. And you?
Sarah: I'm fine, thanks. How can I help you today?
Mr. Wilson: I have questions about my account.

Conversation 4
Christine: Hey, Mark.
Mark: Hey, Christine. How's it going?
Christine: Great. Mark, this is my friend Jean Luc. Jean Luc, Mark's in my English class.
Mark: Sorry. What's your name?
Jean Luc: Jean Luc. I'm from France.
Mark: Oh! Well, it's nice to meet you, Jean Luc.
Jean Luc: Nice to meet you, too, Mark.

Track 03

first, second, third, fourth, fifth, sixth, seventh, eighth, ninth, tenth, eleventh, twelfth, thirteenth, fourteenth, fifteenth, sixteenth, seventeenth, eighteenth, nineteenth, twentieth, twenty-first, twenty-second, twenty-third, twenty-fourth, twenty-fifth, twenty-sixth, twenty-seventh, twenty-eighth, twenty-ninth, thirtieth

Track 04

Olivia: Is registration open?
Registrar: Yes, it is.
Olivia: Great. I want to register for the marathon.
Registrar: What is your first name?
Olivia: Olivia.
Registrar: What's your last name?
Olivia: Lopez.
Registrar: What is your date of birth?
Olivia: October 17, 1999.
Registrar: What's your home address?
Olivia: 45 Third Avenue, Apartment 701.
Registrar: And your phone number?
Olivia: 555-367-5823.
Registrar: It's $25 to register for the marathon.
Olivia: OK. Here's 25.
Registrar: Thanks. OK, you're in group 3. Group 3 starts at 7:45.
Olivia: Thanks.
Registrar: Is this your first marathon?
Olivia: No, it's my fourth!
Registrar: Good luck!

Track 05

Social Media Profile Tips

Many social media websites have different parts in the personal profile section. One part is often about specific preferences—movies, books, TV shows, and sports. Another part is for biographical information. When you create a social media profile, here are some things to consider:

- Are your preferences interesting?
- Is your personal information interesting? Write one or two interesting things about yourself!
- Is your information safe? Don't write your home address, phone number, or vacation dates.
- Are your grammar and spelling correct? Your language is part of your reputation!
- Finally, is your picture good? Use a clear picture of yourself.

Unit 2

Track 01

A Woman at Work: Zinah Saleh, Iraq

Zinah Saleh is a business owner with a successful business. She is the owner of her company, Ishtar Handmade Soap. Her company makes eco-friendly soap and shampoo. The all-natural soap products are very popular. All of the products use olive oil from Iraq. They also use fruit from trees in Africa.

Female business owners are unusual in Iraq. Zinah has a degree in business administration, and she wants to help women find jobs. Zinah's employees are all women. There are female soap makers, administrators, and marketers. Zinah's parents are happy for her. Her father is an engineer and her mother is a homemaker. Zinah thinks working women are important for her country's economy.

Track 02

an architect
an art teacher
an economist
an engineer
an interior designer
an interpreter
an office manager
an optometrist

Track 03

This is Sherry's family. Alicia is Sherry's mother. Tim is her father. Eric is her husband. Her children are Ellie and Danny. Danny is her son and Ellie is her daughter. Her aunts are Cindy and Patricia. Ray is her uncle. John and Kayla are her cousins. Paul is her brother. Lynn is her sister. Mylie is her niece. Billy is her nephew.

Track 04

Sarah: Before we visit your family on Saturday, remind me of who's who.
Alan: OK. My parents' names are Linda and Steve. I have two brothers and a sister.
Sarah: Right. And what are their names?
Alan: Kevin, Robert, and Mary.
Sarah: How old are they?
Alan: Kevin is 28, Mary is 22, and Robert is 17.
Sarah: Are they married?
Alan: Kevin is. He and his wife, Kaitlyn, have a little daughter—my niece, Mindy. Mary isn't married, but she has a boyfriend. His name is Tommy. Of course, Robert isn't married.
Sarah: Well, I'm excited, but I'm a little nervous!
Alan: Don't worry, Sarah. They're all really nice people.

Track 05

Molly: Look at this picture.
Trevor: What a great picture! Who are they?
Molly: It's my Aunt Elsa, Uncle Pete, and my cousins Jeff and Laurie.
Trevor: Where are they?
Molly: They're on vacation in Italy.
Trevor: How cool! So, how old are your cousins?
Molly: Jeff and I are the same age. We're 24. Laurie's 21.
Trevor: What do your aunt and uncle do?
Molly: Aunt Elsa is a pharmacist, and Uncle Pete is a pilot.
Trevor: What do your cousins do?
Molly: Laurie's a student. She's in medical school. Jeff is a computer technician.
Trevor: They're a nice family.
Molly: Yes, they are.

Track 06

Careers Profile
Name: David Monetti
For each category, choose two areas that describe your interests and abilities.
Personality: organized, friendly, patient, independent
Natural abilities: verbal, logical/mathematical, creative, social
Academic skills: science and math, language, technology, arts
Careers Profile Results
High school English teacher
Job description: Teach grammar, writing, and literature. Patience, good communications skills, and IT/social media skills are necessary.

Journalist for city newspaper
Job description: Talk to people and write stories. Need good English and computer skills. We want a creative, independent person.

Computer technician for large company
Job description: Work with computers and help people with computer problems. Lots of travel. A science and engineering education is required.

Marketer for small communications company
Job description: Need a friendly, creative, social person. Good computer and social media skills are necessary. Art or design education is not necessary, but good writing is very important.

Unit 3

Track 01

New Frisbee Champions! Here is an interview with Chris Watson, one half of the Chris–Otto Frisbee team. Chris and Otto are this year's winners.
Interviewer: Congratulations, Chris! You and Otto are the winners! Do you have time to talk to me?
Chris: Sure, thanks. Otto is a great Frisbee player! He runs really fast, and he always catches the Frisbee. Otto loves Frisbee, too. We practice together every day.
Interviewer: Does he like other outdoor activities?
Chris: Well, yes, he likes hiking, but he doesn't like hiking in cold weather.
Interviewer: Does he have any special likes or dislikes?
Chris: Yes, he does. He loves watching TV. He watches soccer and football with me a lot. I like golf, but Otto thinks it's boring. I don't watch it often. And … let's see. He likes eating—a lot! And he hates cats!
Interviewer: Thanks, Chris. Good luck to you and Otto next season.
Chris: Thanks.
Otto: Woof!

Track 02

sounds like /s/: likes, hates, walks, thinks
sounds like /z/: loves, swims, plays, runs
sounds like /iz/: watches, uses, practices, catches

Track 03

Rob: Hey, Sandy. Listen to this!
Sandy: What?
Rob: Shawn Mendes, in concert, here in Denver!
Sandy: When?
Rob: November third. It's a Friday.
Sandy: Cool! Where's the concert?
Rob: City Auditorium. It starts at eight. Do you want to go?
Sandy: Of course I want to go! Please get me a ticket!
Rob: OK. The tickets are $45. Is that OK?
Sandy: That's fine. I can pay you for it before you go.
Rob: OK. Don't forget to write down the information.
Sandy: Sure. Tell me the date again, please.
Rob: November 3, 8:00 p.m., City Auditorium. Got it?
Sandy: Yeah, thanks. Awesome!

Track 04

The City Festival is here! Some of the most popular events are the pet parade, the 10-kilometer race, the dance contest, and of course, the rock concert. Don't forget the bicycle race, the kids' soccer game, and many other fun events!

Festival activities are from 9:00 a.m. to 9:00 p.m. every day this week. Join us and support our festival! Bring your family! Pets are welcome. Buy your tickets online for a discount.

Track 05

Get Together
Name of group: Music Lovers
Do you love music? Do you sing or play an instrument? This is the group for you! We like to go to concerts together, but we LOVE to make our own music!
Name of group: Latinos Play
We are a group of students from Latin American countries. We like eating food from our countries and meeting other Latin American students here in Los Angeles. If you speak Spanish and love good food, join our group!

How to join Get Together
Register for free. Then click on your interests and read about local groups. The members of the groups meet and do different activities. Join the groups that interest you.
How to create a Get Together group
You can start your own Get Together group. Click on "Create a Group." Enter your location. Click on your interest for the new group. Choose a title for the group. Write a short profile of the group. Click "Create Group."

Unit 4

Track 01
The Daily Blog: A Day in the Life of a Reporter

I'm a reporter. I work for an entertainment magazine in New York City. My friends think my job is amazing because I meet famous people. But this is my typical day.

I get up at about 6:30 a.m., and then I walk my dog, have coffee, and get ready for work. I leave home at 7:15 a.m. and I take the subway to my office. I start work at 8:00 a.m. I don't eat breakfast at home because I don't have time. I buy something at the café in the subway station. At work, I go to meetings and write articles for the magazine. I also make a lot of phone calls to get interviews with people. The interviews are interesting, but sometimes the people I interview aren't very friendly or they don't have time to talk.

In the evening, I go home and walk my dog again. Then, I have dinner and watch TV for about two hours. I go to bed at about 10:00 p.m. On weekends I go out with friends, go shopping, or go to a movie.

Track 02
1. What do you do?
2. Where do you live?
3. Why do you like your job?
4. When do you go on vacation?
5. How do you get to class?

Track 03
Marco: This is a conversation with actress Audrey Lang. Audrey, people think that actors have very exciting lives. Is that true?
Audrey: Believe it or not, acting is hard work. We usually work a lot of hours, and most of us don't often go to parties or out with friends.
Marco: What time do you usually start work?
Audrey: Well, we often start at about 6:00 a.m., but sometimes we start later.
Marco: Six o'clock is really early! What time do you finish?
Audrey: We frequently finish at eight or nine at night. It's a long day, and I'm always tired!
Marco: Wow! When do you have days off?
Audrey: I almost always have weekends off. I rarely work on Saturdays, and I never work on Sundays.
Marco: So what do you do on the weekend?
Audrey: Oh, I do things with my family. We almost always go to the supermarket on Saturdays or Sundays. We take the kids to a movie, go to the zoo, or just hang out at home. Four times a year we go to San Francisco to see my parents.
Marco: That sounds like a very normal life.
Audrey: Yes, it is. I know that my job is kind of unusual, but my routine is normal. I get up, I go to work, I come home, we have dinner and talk, or watch TV, and then we go to bed.
Marco: OK. Audrey, thank you for your time.
Audrey: You're welcome.

Track 04
Justin: I'm Justin Watts, and this is *Tell Me About It*. Today our callers tell us if their perfect day off is crazy or lazy! Here's our first caller. Good morning. What's your name?
Brendon: Brendon Novak.
Justin: Thanks for calling, Brendon. What's your favorite type of day off?
Brendon: I get up really late. Then I usually just hang out at home and watch TV or play video games.
Justin: OK, so Brendon really likes relaxing on his days off. Thanks, Brendon. Our next caller is Carla DePalma. Hi, Carla. What kind of day off do you like?
Carla: Hi, Justin. I always do a lot of things on my days off. I take a shower, get dressed, and cook a big breakfast. I almost always do housework in the morning. I sometimes go shopping in the afternoon. I often go out with friends in the evening.
Justin: Carla really likes being active! Thanks, Carla. The next caller is Ali Demir. Hey, Ali. Tell us about your perfect day off.
Ali: I love sports and exercise. On a perfect day, I go to the gym in the morning. I have lunch around 12, and I play soccer with my friends in the afternoon. Then, we usually hang out and watch the other soccer games. In the evening, I do housework and cook dinner.
Justin: That's a busy day off! Thanks, Ali. Our last caller is Melissa Martinez. What's your perfect day off, Melissa?
Melissa: I usually hang out at home and read or listen to podcasts. I sometimes take a nap in the afternoon. I rarely go out, but sometimes friends come over and watch a movie on TV.
Justin: OK, it's a relaxing day for Melissa. That's it for our show until next week!

Track 05
I Need Advice!

I'm 25, and I live in Tampa, Florida, with my two friends Joe and Mario. I have a good job. I'm a nurse, and I work at a big hospital. My work schedule is 9:00 to 5:00 Monday through Friday. I eat lunch in the hospital cafeteria at 1:00 p.m. every day. I always go to the gym after work. In the evening, my roommates and I cook dinner—usually pasta or burgers. We watch TV for about two hours, and I almost always go to bed at about 10:30 p.m. On Saturdays, I go to the gym in the morning and go shopping or do housework in the afternoon. On Saturday evenings, my roommates and I usually order pizza and watch movies. On Sundays, I always play soccer with my friends in the afternoon. I have a very good life—nice friends and a good job, but I'm kind of bored. What do you recommend?

Unit 5

Track 01
Places We Live

For many young people, the idea of buying a home is important. But what happens when you don't have a lot of money to buy? Here are two interesting options for millennials.

Oscar Knight lives in a new apartment in an exciting neighborhood in London. "This is an apartment building designed for young people between the ages of 20 and 35," he says. "We live, work, and play all in one space. It's not boring at all! There are different spaces for us to use, such as a library, a community garden, a gym, an office, a popular restaurant, and a grocery store."

"London is expensive," says Layla, one of Oscar's neighbors. "But it's a fun city. I pay £330 per week here, but that includes Wi-Fi, electricity, water, and a gym. I never feel bored here. It's a great place to live. And the people are very friendly."

Jay Nilsson, from Sweden, lives in an unusual house. He has a one-room eco-pod. "This eco-pod is great," says Jay. "You can live wherever you want. My eco-pod is in my parents' yard on a quiet street. But I can move my eco-pod, too." Eco-pods are not cheap—Jay's eco-pod cost him almost $93,000 dollars. They are also very small—only 8 meters long. But there is a bed, a bathroom, and a tiny kitchen. It's good for one person only!

Track 02

1 lively, quiet, busy
2 expensive, exciting, important

Track 03

1 expensive houses
2 an exciting city
3 busy neighborhood

Track 04

Host: So, the question this morning is "Are there things to do or places to hang out in your neighborhood?" On the line we have … Elsa. Hi, Elsa. Tell us about where you live.

Elsa: Hi there. Well, I live in a neighborhood outside the city of Cartagena, Colombia. It's a boring place to live because it's very quiet and there are no places to hang out. There is a grocery store and a park where old people hang out, but there's no gym and no library. I go to downtown Cartagena to hang out with my friends. There are two areas I like—San Diego and Getsemani. They are popular with university students, and the area is very lively!

Host: Thank you, Elsa. Cartagena sounds like a fun place. Next, we have Ahmed. Ahmed, what is your neighborhood like for young people?

Ahmed: Hello. I'm from Cairo. I live near the city center in a big apartment building. My neighborhood—Zamalek—is an island. It's not busy. There's a high school, and there's a coffee shop where I hang out with my friends. Sometimes we meet in the main square, called Tahrir Square, and walk to the Nile River. It takes about 10 minutes. I like Zamalek a lot.

Host: Thank you, Ahmed. I love Cairo, too. It's a very noisy but interesting city.

Track 05

Conversation 1

A: Excuse me. I'm looking for my friend's apartment. He lives on the corner of Jackson Street and Ninth Avenue.
B: That's easy—just take the second left.
A: Great, thanks.

Conversation 2

A: Hi. Is there a bus stop near here?
B: Yes, there is. It's across from the park.
A: Oh, right. Thanks!

Conversation 3

A: I want to get to … uh … Central Station.
B: Cross the bridge and go straight.
A: Where do I get a ticket?
B: You can get it on the train.
A: OK. Thank you.

Conversation 4

A: I'm lost! Where is the grocery store?
B: It's on the left.
A: No, it's not. There's a restaurant on my left.
B: Oh. Well … turn around.
A: Oh, I see! Thanks!

Conversation 5

A: How do I get to the beach?
B: Follow signs for the airport.
A: The airport?
B: Yes, that's right. The beach is next to the airport. It's a noisy beach!

Track 06

A New Place to Call Home

Name: Katy Morgan

From: Austin, Texas

I'm Katy. I'm from the United States, but now I live in a small neighborhood outside Cusco, Peru. Cusco is an amazing city. Machu Picchu is very close by. I have my own business here. I organize eco-tours around the area.

Life in Peru is great. I speak Spanish, so communication isn't a problem. There are other differences. In the States, things happen fast and people run from place to place. Here, life is slow, and I like it that way!

My neighborhood is small, but there are stores, restaurants (amazing food!), and a beautiful main square (the Plaza de Armas) in the city center. I live in a one-bedroom apartment on a quiet street. There's a small coffee shop across from my house, so I hang out with my neighbors before work. People here like to get together and talk.

It's hard to find a place to live when you arrive in a new city. There's a great company called Home Abroad Rentals. They find apartments for people from other countries who are new to Cusco. They match people to the right home. I'm happy Cusco is the place I call home.

Unit 6

Track 01

Social Media Use and Employment

Do some things about social media make you angry? If your answer is "yes," read on …

Young adults are spending a lot of time on social media these days. According to Statista, about 2.5 billion people use social media. Are you surprised? That's about one-third of the world's population! In the US, around 98% of people aged 16 to 24 have social media accounts. On average, they spend 109 minutes per day—almost two hours—on social media. China has more social media users than any other country—596 million. That number is growing all the time.

Many people are afraid that employers are getting information about them from social media. This information can make them feel embarrassed.

A study by Statista from 2017 shows that 61% of employers look at social media profiles before they hire someone. So, be very careful and check your settings. Keep your social media profiles for family and friends only.

Track 02

Speaker 1

Yeah, I vlog every two or three days. Right now, I'm using my laptop to upload videos, but I usually use my smartphone. I think you get good pictures of the vegetables on it. My favorite? In my opinion, peppers. I love them!

Speaker 2

Well, it's my job and my hobby. I'm a travel writer for a magazine. I spend about six months of the year away from home. I'm staying in a very big hotel in Colorado now. It has 1,500 rooms! I love vlogging. I'm not just looking at a computer all day. I'm talking to people all over the world.

Speaker 3

I'm a college student. I'm studying to be a computer programmer. I make money by showing gamers how to play video games. In my opinion, all you need is a good desktop computer or a laptop, a webcam, and some headphones. I think vlogging is cool.

Speaker 4

I love shopping. The fact is people always ask me for advice on what to buy. I vlog about all the good and bad things I buy, like clothes, smartphones, beauty products—anything, really! In my view, helping people make decisions about what to buy is important.

Track 03

1 I think you get good pictures of the vegetables on it.
2 The fact is people always ask me for advice on what to buy.
3 In my opinion, all you need is a good desktop computer or a laptop, a webcam, and some headphones.
4 I'm staying in a very big hotel in Colorado now. It has 1,500 rooms!
5 In my view, helping people make decisions about what to buy is important.

Track 04

Host: Hello and welcome to *Digital Life*. With me today is Luca Morris, a 20-year-old entrepreneur from Toronto, Canada. Hi, Luca.
Luca: Hello.
Host: Now, tell us, what do you do?
Luca: Well, I sell athletic shoes.
Host: But not in a store, right?
Luca: No! I sell my athletic shoes online.
Host: So, how does it work? How do you make money?
Luca: Well, I go online and buy regular athletic shoes. Then I customize them. That means I make every pair look different. I add lots of colors and interesting designs on them.
Host: And then you sell them?
Luca: Yes. I usually add about $40 or $50 to my cost.
Host: Sounds easy! And how do actually sell your shoes?
Luca: I have a website. You can also download an app for buying and selling things online. I use that sometimes.
Host: I see.
Luca: I upload pictures of new shoes every two or three days. Sometimes I wear the shoes, take a selfie, and use that picture to update my profile. Or I take videos. People like that. I hope my videos go viral!
Host: OK.
Luca: When I add new shoes, I send a message to all my customers.
Host: And are your shoes popular?
Luca: I think so! People post comments about them online. They usually say good things.
Host: Is this an easy business?
Luca: Well, it takes a lot of my time. But I have a day job, too—I work in a restaurant.
Host: And what about the future?
Luca: Well, my business is growing. If I go viral, I can quit my day job.
Host: Good luck, Luca! Thanks for coming in.

Track 05

1 I send a message to all my customers.
2 I upload pictures of new shoes every two or three days.
3 People post comments about them online.
4 … update my profile …
5 If I go viral, I can quit my day job.
6 Sometimes I wear the shoes, take a selfie, and use that picture…

Track 06

1 kin, king   2 sin, sing   3 thin, thing

Track 07

1 Sing this song.
2 The teacher is talking.
3 I'm listening to music.

Track 08

How to Do a Digital Detox

Are you spending too much time using your phone? Check the things that are true for you to find out:

- I check social media before I get out of bed.
- I send messages while I have breakfast.
- I often take my phone to the bathroom.
- I never go out without my phone.

Did you check three or four? Then it may be time for a digital detox. Mandy Morgan, a social media expert, gives us this advice …

"This isn't about tech devices," she explains, "it's about understanding what is healthy. People usually feel good when they don't use their smartphones all the time."

Morgan says that a seven-day detox helps with your sleep, your studies and how you feel. She asks people to check their screen time and count how many times a day they pick up their phone.

When you do a digital detox, you don't have your phone all the time. For seven days, you practice when and where you use your smartphone. You learn to leave your phone at home sometimes.

Marcia Estefan (DJ Blade), 23, is a club DJ from Brasilia. She is also studying to be a doctor. "I use my phone all the time," she explains. "I never think about how often I look at my screen." These days Marcia doesn't use her phone often. She rarely takes it out with her in the evening. "It makes me think about how I use technology and that's a good thing."

Before the Digital Detox:
Screen Time Per Day: 3 hours 20 minutes
Picks Up Her Phone: 56 times a day
After the Digital Detox:
Screen Time Per Day: 1 hour 50 minutes

Macmillan Education Limited
4 Crinan Street
London N1 9XW

Companies and representatives throughout the world

Speak Your Mind Level 1A Student's Book
ISBN 978-138-003-109-9
Speak Your Mind Level 1A Student's Book + access to Student's App and Digital Workbook ISBN 978-138-003-108-2
Speak Your Mind Level 1A Student's Book + access to Student's App
ISBN 978-138-003-107-5

Written by Mickey Rogers, Joanne Taylore-Knowles, and Steve Taylore-Knowles

The authors have asserted their right to be identified as the authors of this work in accordance with the Copyright, Designs, and Patents Act 1988.

First published 2020

Designed by QBS Learning
Illustrated by Lon Eric Craven (Wendy Lynn & Co.) p. 42; Daniel Deamo (Lemonade Illustration) p. 21; QBS Learning pp. 41, 52, 140.
Original cover design by therestless.co.uk
Cover adaptation by Roberto Martinez
Cover photographs by **Getty Images**/PeopleImages (upper body), Getty Images/Tim Robberts (lower body), Getty Images/Chatuporn Sornlampoo/EyeEm (background); **Shutterstock**/REDPIXEL.PL (window).
Picture research by Fernanda Rocha/Ikonia LLC

Authors' acknowledgements
Mickey, Jo and Steve would like to thank everyone at Macmillan Education and RedNova Learning who have made this project possible and who have gone the extra mile (literally!) to meet up, work together, and throw around a million ideas, some of which even made their way into the books! Jo and Steve would also like to thank Scout for her patience and understanding and for letting her parents get on with it when they needed to!

The publishers would like to thank all the teachers that piloted and reviewed the series, and a special thanks to Annette Flavel for content and cultural reviews.

The authors and publishers would like to thank the following for permission to reproduce their photographs:
Alamy Stock Photo/Blend Images p. 50(4); **Getty Images**/Blend Images p. 50(5), Getty Images/Brand X Pictures/Hero Images p. 20(Alicia), Getty Images/Peter Cade p. 30, Getty Images/Caialmage/Dan Dalton, Getty Images/Caialmage/Tom Merton p. 40(t), Getty Images/Caiaimage/Chris Ryan p. 19, Getty Images/DigitalVision/Hill Street Studios LLC p. 20(Billy), Getty Images/DigitalVision/Lucy Lambriex p. 10(m), Getty Images/Dina Belenko Photography p. 131, Getty Images/elenaleonova p. 42(7), Getty Images/E+/AIMSTOCK p. 22(5), Getty Images/E+/Yuri_Arcurs p. 20(Tim), Getty Images/E+/asiseeit p. 12, Getty Images/E+/fotografixx p. 48(l), Getty Images/E+/xavierarnau p. 20(Mike), Getty Images/Hero Images pp. 20(Ray, Kayla), 22(1,8), Getty Images/Corey Hochachka/Design Pics p. 22(b), Getty Images/Hoxton/Ryan Lees p. 20(Paul), Getty Images/ibreakstock p. 28, Getty Images/iStock/artisteer p. 63(A), Getty Images/iStock/cinoby p. 50(br), Getty Images/iStock/Antonio_Diaz p. 60(2b), Getty Images/iStock/DMEPhotography p. 14(bl), Getty Images/iStock/jenifoto p. 55(b), Getty Images/iStock/Pinkypills p. 22(3), Getty Images/iStock/silverkblack p. 60(4b), Getty Images/iStock/tiler84 p. 32(b), Getty Images/iStock/TommL p. 132, Getty Images/iStock/ViewApart pp. 34, Getty Images/iStock/YinYang p. 20(Cindy), Getty Images/Jetta Productions Inc. pp. 22(7), 50(8), Getty Images/JGI/Jamie Grill p. 42(8), Getty Images/John & Lisa Merrill p. 32, Getty Images/Johner Images p. 50(2), Getty Images/Jesse Kraft/EyeEm p. 50(bl), Getty Images/Kirsty Lee/EyeEm p. 60(6), Getty Images/LWA p. 22(4), Getty Images/Emilija Manevska p. 60(5), Getty Images/martin-dm p. 60(3b), Getty Images/Maskot p. 55(l), Getty Images/michaeljung p. 35(b), Getty Images/Dimitri Otis p. 20(Lynne), Getty Images/Chonlachai Panprommas/EyeEm p. 60(1t), Getty Images/Jose Luis Pelaez Inc. p. 22(2), Getty Images/Jessica Peterson p. 20(Sherry, John), Getty Images/PhotoAlto/Alix Minde p. 60(4t), Getty Images/Science Photo Library p. 60(3t), Getty Images/SSC p. 42(3), Getty Images/Alex Tihonovs/EyeEm p. 50(6), Getty Images/Siwabud Veerapaisarn/EyeEm p. 46, Getty Images/Bogdan Vija/EyeEm p. 20(Danny), Getty Images/Dougal Waters p. 42(5), Getty Images/Westend61 pp. 17, 20(Ellie, Mylie), 23(cl, insets), 27, Getty Images/Stephen Zeigler p. 20(Eric), Getty Images/10'000 Hours p. 58; **Shutterstock**/andregric p. 62, Shutterstock/antoniodiaz p. 42(2), Shutterstock/Radu Bercan p. 7, Shutterstock/Billion Photos pp. 56, 129, Shutterstock/Farknot Architect p. 60(2t), Shutterstock/first vector trend p. 127(tr), Shutterstock/flower travelin' man pp. 28, 58, Shutterstock/Art_Photo p. 10(r), Shutterstock/Bobex-73 p. 31, Shutterstock/cretolamna p. 28(inset), Shutterstock/DisobeyArt p. 57, Shutterstock/Dean Drobot p. 44, Shutterstock/Ekaterina Markelova p. 64, Shutterstock/ESB Professional pp. 6, 55(r), Shutterstock/Rainer Fuhrmann p. 37, Shutterstock/Grigvovan p. 42(1), Shutterstock/Antonio Guillem p. 24, Shutterstock/Jirsak p. 66, Shutterstock/Lightspring pp. 16, 127(m), Shutterstock/Ocskay Mark p. 8, Shutterstock/GANNA MARTYSHEVA p. 40(b), Shutterstock/Monkey Business Images pp. 42(4), 50(1,7), 130, Shutterstock/Mr Z p. 43, Shutterstock/Photographee.eu p. 35(t), Shutterstock/Andrey_Popov p. 22(6), Shutterstock/Prostock-studio p. 47, Shutterstock/sirtravelalot p. 10(l), Shutterstock/Terdsak L p. 128, Shutterstock/Syda Productions p. 60(7,8), Shutterstock/Vlad Teodor p. 53, Shutterstock/UfaBizPhotoz p. 42(6), Shutterstock/Vgstockstudio p. 38, Shutterstock/YAKOBCHUK VIACHESLAV p. 60(1b), Shutterstock/Dmytro Zinkevych p. 127(m); **Superstock**/Matt Dutile/Image Source p. 54; **123RF**/Mariia Loginova p. 63(B), 123RF/Andriy Popov p. 50(3).63(B), 123RF/Andriy Popov p. 50(3).

Additional Sources:
p. 26, "Malicious bot traffic climbs 9.5 percent in 2017, says report," by Bradley Barth, March 27, 2018, SC Media website. p. 26, "34 Interesting Facts about Computer Virus," by Preeti Seth, April 25, 2019, Tweak Library website. p. 56, *UNESCO Science Report*, 2019, UNESCO website; "Few Students Likely to Use Print Books for Research," by Drew DeSilver, July 30, 2013, Pew Research Center website. p. 56, "For 53% Reliable Information, Click Here," by Dan Ackman, January 31, 2003, *Forbes*. p. 66, "101 Interesting Facts about Digital Marketing," by Vincent Wee, April 28, 2016, Tech Edt website. p. 66, "The 25 Best Cities for Marketing Jobs in 2017," Best Marketing Degrees website, 2017.

Printed and bound in Argentina

2021
10